SCHOOL CRISIS CASE STUDIES, VOLUME 2

BEFORE ANOTHER SCHOOL SHOOTING OCCURS

Helen M. Sharp

Rowman & Littlefield Education
A division of
Rowman & Littlefield Publishers, Inc.
Lanham • New York • Toronto • Plymouth, UK

Published by Rowman & Littlefield Education
A division of Rowman & Littlefield Publishers, Inc.
A wholly owned subsidiary of The Rowman & Littlefield Publishing Group, Inc.
4501 Forbes Boulevard, Suite 200, Lanham, Maryland 20706
http://www.rowmaneducation.com

Estover Road, Plymouth PL6 7PY, United Kingdom

British Library Cataloguing in Publication Information Available

Library of Congress Cataloging-in-Publication Data

Sharp, Helen M.
  School crisis case studies : before another school shooting occurs / Helen M.
Sharp.
    p. cm.
  ISBN 978-1-60709-151-6 (cloth : alk. paper) — ISBN 978-1-60709-152-3 (pbk.
: alk. paper) — ISBN 978-1-60709-153-0 (electronic)
  1. School crisis management—Case studies. 2. School violence—Prevention—
Case studies. I. Title.
  LB2866.5.S46 2009
  371.7'820973—dc22   2009024722

∞™ The paper used in this publication meets the minimum requirements of
American National Standard for Information Sciences—Permanence of Paper
for Printed Library Materials, ANSI/NISO Z39.48-1992.
Manufactured in the United States of America.

Printed in the United States of America

CONTENTS

PREFACE

No school is immune from crisis situations.

Creating and maintaining safe schools is a primary responsibility for contemporary school personnel, led by school leaders who may promote changes in current policies and practices related specifically to safety issues. Some of these crisis events are described in this book.

School Crisis Case Studies, vol. 2, enables future and current school leaders to review the cases provided and assess effective responses to each crisis in the context of the schools with which the leader is most familiar.

Because school leaders make it a priority to implement and maintain safe school practices, this book offers a review of critical incidents. If changes in current policies and practices occur following a reader's review of these cases, students and all members of the school community will benefit.

A safe school is an expectation of parents, students, administrators, board members, and the public. Can students learn in any environment other than a safe one? Preparation for school safety begins with reading these cases and directing attention to safe school issues in the buildings the administrator knows best.

FOREWORD: SCHOOL CRISIS PLANNING

A School Leader's Perspective

Thomas Kopetskie

If one were to say that change occurs in public education circles at glacial speed, that would be unfair to the glaciers. Typically, unless they have been compelled to change by outside forces—often governmental, as in No Child Left Behind—public schools have remained basically unchanged since the 1950s. Some of the buildings, particularly high schools, even look the same as they did when our grandparents attended school. One dramatic exception to this paradigm, however, is clearly manifested in the area of school safety.

School safety includes actions relative to crisis preparation, prevention, and management. Both prior to and after the notorious Columbine tragedy in April 1999, American schools across the country have been subject to periodic school emergency situations involving violence in one form or another. Educational administrators and staff members are on notice to be vigilant and attend seriously to crisis planning. Those who fail to heed this warning are destined to repeat the mistakes made by others before them.

The sad fact is violent acts in schools can occur anywhere, at any time. Events in the bucolic area surrounding Lancaster, Pennsylvania, over a period of just five years are dire proof, validating this assertion. It is an understatement to say that tragic events have regularly visited this once-serene location.

Starting in February 2001, with a machete attack on an elementary school principal, an onslaught of tragedies visited this remote area, located far from any major urban center. A follow-up situation occurred in nearby Red Lion schools in April, 2003: a disturbed middle school student shot and killed his principal. The most chilling event of all, however, occurred in October 2006, when a deranged gunman entered a peaceful Amish schoolhouse, taking the young teacher and her class hostage. He eventually slaughtered several female students, while severely maiming others. The gunman, who shot himself as well, apparently did not know any of his victims.

Truly, if such wanton violence can occur among "the gentle people" in Amish country, violence can be perpetrated anywhere. Unfortunately, there are too many other examples of school violence to cite in a single chapter. Suffice it to say that no school, public or private, is immune from violence; and in these troubled times, taking prudent and necessary precautions is a matter of life and death.

Volumes have been written about many of these school tragedies, and even the FBI and the Secret Service have weighed in on the topic of targeted violence in schools. These experts have expressed divergent views and mixed commentary about whether a stereotypical profile of a school shooter exists. What they all agree upon is that in every case, classmates of student offenders have stated that they themselves failed to report threats to school personnel. It seems they were not acclimated to taking such threats seriously. Countless lives have been altered and many lost as a result of this single factor.

This foreword investigates major changes that are the direct results of myriad school tragedies that took place in the last decade. Warning signs can no longer be overlooked; but even more tragic would be a wasted opportunity to thoroughly plan for the worst that could happen. On the basis of the crisis situations that we know have occurred in recent years, we cannot let an opportunity pass by to address school crisis situations. To do so would be nothing short of deliberate indifference and a callous invitation for calamity.

EARLY ATTEMPTS AT SCHOOL SAFETY

Until the catastrophe at Columbine culminated a series of late-1990s school shootings, efforts to insulate schools were basically hit-or-miss. Only the most forward thinking of school leaders imagined it "could happen here." Furthermore, very few schools in each state were eligible to receive federal funding under the Safe and Drug Free school grants then available. Far too often, because these monies were extended by need, schools with poor violence statistics that improved in the first year of the grant were denied follow-up funds. These Safe and Drug Free grants were typically earmarked for the purchase of equipment, services, and materials to make schools safer.

Looking back, it seems as though it took multiple nationwide incidents to raise the level of concern in all communities regarding funding of local school-safety efforts. It is now hard to believe that the mere idea of having police officers in or near school campuses was taboo, and was rejected outright by local school boards in all but the most urban of school settings.

The fact remains clear: the noteworthy instances of school violence in the late 1990s did not occur in large cities, but rather in places such as Pearl, Mississippi; West Paducah, Kentucky; Jonesboro, Arkansas; Edinboro, Pennsylvania; and Springfield, Oregon, in 1997 and 1998. On April 20, 1999, the tragedy in Littleton, Colorado, proved that even elite communities were not immune to school violence.

Events at Columbine touched off a nationwide mania of vain attempts to identify common characteristics of perpetrators in a profile. Sadly, this diversion may have wasted valuable time—the ages, personalities, and motivations of school shooters varied markedly. Worse yet, the overemphasis on the *who* carried a risk of oversimplifying and, in some instances, overidentifying. Eventually, authorities concluded that approaches based on fact and communication were more productive than those based on character traits. The bottom line was energy, and school resources were most prudently funneled to preventive measures.

Schools started to take the business of planning to protect students and staff into their own hands, even if only by conducting random checks with metal detectors at school-entry locations. Though not a contributing factor in every instance of school violence, the topic of bullying hit center stage and drew significant attention. This was clearly evidenced by the sharp increase in the number of prepackaged antibullying programs offered for sale to schools. It was folly, however, to be deluded into thinking a "one-size-fits-all" antiviolence package would or should meet the needs across the school spectrum in such a diverse nation. Ultimately, plans developed locally and customized by in-house personnel proved much more efficient and effective. These measures opened the door for the development of safety-net practices to meet unique local needs better than they could be met by the expensive, generic safety plans flooding the open market.

THE EVOLUTION OF SAFETY PLANS

Perhaps the single most successful measure taken by schools to thwart school violence was the institution of building-based and districtwide crisis teams. With the safety of all students and staff as their sole priority, these localized teams established viable procedures and measures so that all school staff members were knowledgeable and were prepared to respond to a variety of potential emergency situations.

Many schools chose to dispense binders or even flip charts enumerating timely actions for a host of potential crises. The development of consistent, structured sets of plans did much to raise the level of concern and, more importantly, the level of confidence in addressing dangerous situations. A good number of states mandated the development of school safety plans and even the implementation of crisis-planning teams. Some required local school districts to submit their plans for state approval.

A natural progression from written plans and manuals was the actual simulated practice of emergency response by administrators and staff members in fabricated, yet closely monitored, scenarios. Once established, this practice evolved into actual lockdown practice sessions with students, much like the time-honored tradition of monthly evacuation fire drills required by many states. "Perfect practice makes perfect" became the credo in school circles as school personnel and students became familiar with the nuances of the lockdown drill. Preplanning of incident response with students became as much a part of daily school life as teaching them how to answer the questions on all of the state-mandated tests.

Going a step further, several states developed harsh, zero-tolerance weapons policies via legislation. These policies required the expulsion of any student bringing a weapon to school. Local and state police, for their part, did staff in-service training on cults and gang-member identification. They spoke specifically about groups actively present in the local community.

Instead of the denial of the past, a spirit of proactive and preincident planning started to become part and parcel of the school milieu. School boards revisited earlier decisions and reversed policy relative to acceptable school dress—and even uniforms. It is obvious that in many circles, concern about gang apparel and symbolism drew increased attention.

POLICE IN SCHOOLS

As noted previously, the adoption of policies that made police visible in the schools came about slowly. Initially, school officials met with local police representatives to draw up memoranda of understanding. These documents spelled out the relationship between the two entities and enumerated a chain of command and responsibilities in the event of joint actions. This initial step was taken further when several state legislatures offered seed money in order to utilize school police officers as "resource officers."

The chain of command and specific responsibilities in the event of joint actions was a mechanism that appeared predominantly in junior and senior high schools; and, before long, principals wondered aloud how they ever got along without it. Whether armed or not, the police presence sent a clear message: safety was a top priority, and a show of strength would be present at a moment's notice.

According to reports from the Secret Service, incidents of targeted violence in schools were rarely impulsive. Furthermore, their specialists concluded that a readily discernable pattern of behavior leads to violent acts. It was this pattern that school resource officers were trained to be on the alert for. The job required the insight to weed out false signals from fact and an ability to amass intelligence in regard to potentially violent situations. School resource officers (SROs) represent a key piece in the school safety puzzle today.

TECHNOLOGY AND SCHOOL SAFETY

The extensive use of new technology is another abrupt departure from the old days when schools were virtually open to any and all who chose to enter their doors. Initially, random usage of metal detectors occurred with increased frequency. That systematic change broke the ice, leading to an evolution in school entry that is noticeable to anyone attempting to venture into schools.

Credit needs to go to both television and local newspapers for testing the security of school buildings and then admonishing open schools for how easy it was to enter them. Though the negative publicity was embarrassing, the phenomenon of rocks holding doors open in schools became more rare. School personnel started to realize that school safety trumped any personal convenience. Today, teachers are given entry cards or numeric passwords for keypads in order to reenter schools after lunch, recess, or outside gym activities.

There are many other means used to prevent just anyone from sauntering into local school buildings. Cameras and buzz-in switches are standard everywhere. Many schools have door monitors or even their own paid security staff to question entering visitors as they sign them in at the school lobby. Visitors' passes and badges are required, and many schools wand visitors with regularity for weapons. Students and staff receive identification badges, and they are required to show them if they are not attached to their clothing. Alarm systems often partition off isolated areas of buildings before and after the school day.

A recent trend in an increasing number of school districts is the presence of automated computer stations in vestibules. Electronic sign-in of school visitors requires even substitute teachers and parents who regularly volunteer in the schools to supply basic data. These computers take information, including purpose of visit and the name of the person(s) with whom the visitor will meet, and they even generate a photo, which is printed on a specific identification-tag label. For example, in the Wilmington, North Carolina, elementary public schools, the automated school entry has been universally adopted. A side benefit is the time saved by school secretaries, who do not have to stop their work frequently and manage numerous sign-in sheets.

PARENTS AND SCHOOL SAFETY

Clearly, on the whole, parents are welcoming safety measures despite minor inconveniences such as electronic or even paper sign-in at schools. Parents can often helpfully provide tips from overheard conversations and the like. Some schools maintain anonymous tip lines for parents who may not want to be identified, yet have specific concerns.

The National Crime Prevention Council has addressed the role of parents and highlighted what they can do to maintain school safety. Quite simply, the NCPC strongly suggests that parents be ever vigilant by listening closely to their children, especially seeking to elicit any specific safety concerns. The need to monitor computer history and MySpace activity is included in the NCPC's prescription for identifying any red-flag situations. Cyber-bullying is rampant with the advent of technology, and many times such activity spills over into the school. When in doubt, parents need to begin to be comfortable addressing valid safety concerns with school administrators, teachers, and school resource officers.

SCHOOL PUBLIC RELATIONS

Although not perfected by any means, the critical process of schools providing information to their many publics has shown considerable progress, especially regarding information for parents. Larger districts tend to employ public relations specialists to work with local newspapers, television, and radio, and, of course, parent and community-based groups. With increased numbers of students using cell phones, schools have been forced to be proactive in generating information to parents, in particular, when dangerous situations threaten to arise.

Automated phone-call systems save precious time and expedite the passage of important information—and often quell false rumors. In a matter of a few minutes, many parents can hear the same message from a single school source. This process saves countless hours of frantic calls to individuals' homes and cell phones. Though expensive, emergency phone systems have altered the way schools communicate; they are now a cutting-edge necessity. Since all parents may not have access to computers, these phone systems provide the most reliable means to reach them in a timely manner.

WORST-CASE SCENARIOS

Due to human variables and frailties and even just plain bad luck, the cold, hard truth is that sporadic instances of violent acts will continue to occur in school venues. Such tragedies are destined to occur in isolation despite diligent preparation and the most seemingly foolproof preventive measures. As noted already, in each and every case of school violence studied by the FBI and the Secret Service, someone dropped the ball when it came to reporting a potential threat. Prior statements about "getting even" or the desire to exact revenge were not given credence. Sadly, that this will never happen again would be a lot to expect.

Postincident preparation is also a critical area of school safety. What, then, are the essential components when the worst does occur?

Postincident Response Plan

Some key aspects of postcrisis planning mirror the preincident measures addressed previously in this review. Site-level postincident response teams need to be in place, and their members both visible and accessible immediately after the crisis. Their to-do list is comprehensive and critical: hold staff meeting to debrief; coordinate communication processes; dispel rumors; and move the school entity slowly back to "normalcy." The following guidelines should be observed by the response team:

1. Prior to any incidents, address the availability of rooms for staff and students to use to take mental health breaks, and specify the rooms set aside for this purpose.
2. Preplan the types and content of information to be disseminated. Both the press and the public will demand to know the facts, not resting until they receive a plausible explanation.
3. Recognize that a remote command post is a practical need, as are periodic follow-up briefings planned beyond the initial briefing.
4. If a full-time public relations specialist exists, apprise that person of all aspects of crisis situations and anticipated strategies. This is in advance of others on-site, and it should be followed by new information that is provided for dissemination as it becomes available. The public will expect information from this source.
5. Recognize that the emergency phone system is an invaluable resource for relating vital, accurate information to parents swiftly. Above all, regardless of how information is dispensed, anticipate that the public will want to know what occurred and how the situation was handled, as well as what took place in the aftermath of the event.

Employees and Students

According to the FBI, local law-enforcement personnel and school health and guidance staff need to assume a leadership role to meet the needs of school staff and students. Mental-health professionals should be available for those who are in shock or traumatized.

In absolute-worst-case situations involving a loss of life, an extended recovery program is essential. The sudden deaths of students or staff in a single incident will surely touch many peers. A prolonged series of incidents (a series of student suicides, for instance) requires sensitivity and the coordinated efforts of the school with many other agencies. Any death involving a younger person, especially a violent death, shakes the very core of adults as well as students. All these individuals need to try to make sense of the inexplicable and will require some professional assistance to do so.

Getting Back

A central question requiring response by members of the postincident response team will be at what point an attempt might be made to return to normalcy. Each team reflects upon this question in the aftermath of a critical event and creates a viable timeline for the staff and, ultimately, the students. The time of resuming the normal routine varies from one case to another. There is no rule of thumb. Whenever resumption occurs, it should be tightly scheduled and realistic in terms of what one expects to be accomplished.

Students will need assurance that despite what has happened, the school is a secure place for them. Once the initial student-return day is over, it is wise to have faculty and staff meet once again to receive feedback and keep everyone on the same page. Certainly, an increased and visible security presence during the postincident time period is important, both mentally and physically, for all parties.

CONCLUSION

It is not the purpose of this foreword to provide all of the answers, nor to enumerate or outline solutions. Violence in American society has become commonplace, and, inevitably, it has spilled over into an entity that used to be immune from societal violence—that is, the school. Violent behavior and atrocities in schools have been like an infection, attacking all regions of our country at an alarming rate. These are difficult times for students in our schools, as instances of bullying (especially cyberbullying) have clearly prompted the reactions of many and contributed to an increase in violent tendencies.

Despite immense investments of time, money, and planning, we are a long way from making school violence extinct. As long as there is bias or bigotry; physical, psychological, and emotional abuse; alcohol and drug abuse; and the availability of weapons, we can expect people in crisis to follow paths leading to violence.

The various measures outlined in this foreword are important to establishing a safety net of sorts and providing a blueprint for consideration. Each school's professionals need to examine the tools used by others to preplan for students' and adults' unique needs in crisis situations. The ultimate challenge is to find a consensus plan that planning groups can espouse as their own. They need to accomplish this task without going to extremes and negatively impacting their community at large.

Schools are not mini-prisons, yet every school must address these concerns and provide the security needed to promote an environment for academic excellence. Schools with realistic, workable safety plans can mobilize quickly in times of chaos and crisis. At this point, there is really no excuse for a lack of preparedness. As the old adage goes, "Those who fail to learn the lessons of history are doomed to repeat its errors."

1

THE NEW IMPERATIVE
Safe School Behavior, Strategies, and Practices

Is *safety consciousness* part of your school's curriculum? Maybe the time to address school safety is at the start of a new school year, before classes and homework, extracurricular activities and sports, part-time, after-school jobs, or responsibilities at home claim students' attention. Unless adults review, and remind students about, safety issues and potential responses to these issues, we cannot expect them to act appropriately when a safety issue surfaces.

An example of compromising school safety occurs regularly in most schools: Students inside a school building who see a student (or students) on the other side of a door locked on the outside are more likely than not to open the door and let the student or students in. Whether students wave and show they cannot open the door, or shout "Let me in!" they gain access. This occurs even if insiders do not recognize the outsider(s). How safe is that? School adults may not have impressed upon students that it is an unwise decision to open a door to anyone, even a stranger with books. Most likely, students have been told which entrances to use if they must travel between several buildings. There is a lesson here to review with students, along with raising and discussing other school safety issues. Would a review of school safety rules and reminders in an assembly work well, or is the topic best for a classroom session?

Yearly reminders of the school's or district's safety policies and practices, and the penalties and consequences following safe school violations, seem necessary. Parents must also learn about a school's commitment to its students' safety. The local newspaper and television stations might offer school safety officers and their assistants an opportunity to explain school safety rules and the priority of all building adults to maintain a safe campus. What are the alternatives? One alternative might be students' lack of awareness about security issues and procedures, leaving them without recourse should an event surface.

Engaging students in safety awareness and responses to specific incidents may occur in written form, in addition to verbal reminders. A section in the student handbook or a pamphlet about the district's efforts regarding safe school rules might specify concerns and violations. Some specific thoughts follow.

1. Students should report any open but unoccupied classroom to a teacher or the main office.
2. Students should confide in a counselor, the safety officer, a teacher, a coach, or another building adult if they are aware of rumors circulating, particularly rumors about unsafe behavior, a fight or disruption that is planned, or a student carrying a weapon. (How might we convince students to do so?)
3. Students should report any event that they regard as *suspicious* or *unsafe*. For example, a sophomore felt ill during gym and went to the locker room to change clothing and then call home. She found a student checking all the gym lockers, looking for an open one. The intruder may have known that a number of girls left their lockers unlocked during gym class because there was so little time to shower and dress and get to their next class on time. The open lockers allowed students to grab towels and shower accessories more quickly, but leaving a locker unlocked is not a safe behavior.

4. Students should confide in an adult if they overhear or receive a threat of some sort, such as "We need twenty dollars the next time we see you. *Understand?*" An attempt to extort money cannot be taken lightly or ignored. No one in a school setting has the right to intimidate another student in this manner.

5. *Car-hopping* involves students checking cars in the student lot to see if they are open, giving the *hoppers* an opportunity to steal whatever is in the vehicles. Thefts of money or materials from cars should be reported, or else the practice will continue. Vehicle damage is also likely if there are no safety personnel on duty. An adult parking lot monitor may be necessary—to keep outsiders away from cars and prevent them from potentially entering a school building.

6. The school's safety officer might present safety reminders in a number of grade-level meetings or on a local television channel. A quarterly "safe behavior" bulletin of reminders, with a review of any incidents compromising safety and their containment, might also appear in the local newspaper.

7. If a building's atmosphere seems different to an adult—students are nervous, they are unable to pay attention in classes, and they are whispering among themselves—the adult should ask a trusted student what is causing the unusual behaviors. Students may be waiting for an event or disruption to occur. There are usually warning signs, specifically students whispering among themselves in advance of a planned event.

8. Students need to remain alert at all times to any issue, event, or circumstance related to students' and building safety; all those in the building have the obligation to report any suspicions. But how might we convince listeners that "narc-ing" is sometimes required for the safety of all students?

9. Adult monitors should be provided for school buses; middle- and high school students are unruly, if not wild and boisterous, at the end of the school day. We may be entering the time when all school buses have an adult other than the driver to monitor students' behavior. The bus driver is fully occupied with safety and traffic conditions.

10. If a student's emotional well-being is compromised by threats, belittling, taunts, and/or behaviors that attempt to provoke a response, adults should encourage students to report that they have seen or heard about these threats and taunts. Such incidents should be reported to the school safety officer, dean, or principal as soon as possible. No student should endure humiliation or fear at school. All students have an obligation to report every instance of bullying behavior that they have witnessed or experienced themselves. Students need to respect others in all public situations.

11. Upon seeing a stranger (student or adult) in school, a student should talk to the first adult he or she sees and try to pinpoint the individual. Similarly, a student noticing a group of students gathered near the school building but at the required distance from the campus should also report that fact to the safety officer, a teacher, or the building leader. The whole school—adults and students—may be at risk.

12. A student safety group might work with the school safety officer and an administrator to plan a Safety Awareness Day, inviting police or sheriff's deputies to review school safety measures and encourage student compliance, using their experiences. They may become resource personnel, suggesting other measures necessary to the school's current plan.

13. A safe school policy outlining the rights and responsibilities of students should be drafted, and included in the student handbook. Every student's role in maintaining a safe school should be emphasized, with appropriate suggestions (as shown in the items above).

14. Students should be reminded that school safety efforts could involve administrators and/or safety personnel, or police officers and dogs, if necessary, searching any student locker, with no advance warning.

15. Above all, students should remain alert and attentive on campus and in classrooms—to the school's atmosphere, to rumors, to unusual events, to any suspicious activity, to any strangers

in the building, and to any potential destructive behavior or disruptions.

READINESS

1. Review safety issues and strategies and the school rules in each classroom on the opening day of each new school term. Use the first hour of classes, for example. If students engage in discussions about school policies and practices, this is even more beneficial. Take notes on students' concerns. Follow up on questions raised that you were unable to answer. Every teacher will be a safety resource person.
2. All building adults might have a specific security assignment in the school building—to remain with the class being taught when the event occurs, as in a lockdown, or to assist a security-staff member or monitor a specific section of the building with another adult.
3. Allow security staff to contain the safety emergency. Remain on alert for an all-clear message or additional instructions. Or, if told to do so, evacuate the building and assemble at the assigned location outdoors.
4. If told to stay in the classroom, keep students calm, away from windows, and away from the locked door.

RESPONSIBILITY

1. An adult in a classroom is the best source of information about a safety issue, as well as a calming presence. After containment of a problem or event, building leaders announce and explain circumstances as they are able or willing to do so. Advise students that they may not receive all the information they want until authorities and school leaders agree to release it.

2. If asked to maintain a station in the building, take your cell phone. Or you may be asked to join other building adults in a group to rove and/or monitor specific areas. What other school personnel might be called upon to aid in a safety issue? Using all building personnel should guarantee adequate coverage of the campus.

RESPONSE

1. Allow the school security team and its designated school personnel to deal directly with the security issue that arises. They will communicate with local police as needed.
2. Calm students and keep the noise level low; answer questions, assuring students that they are safe in the locked room until the incident is contained or an individual is identified and his or her plan terminated.
3. If you are assigned to inform other adults of the problem in your section of the building or to monitor a specific area, attempt to do with a calm sense of purpose.

2

AN ATMOSPHERE FOR ACADEMIC SUCCESS

P.S. 108, a middle school for grades 6 through 8, looks like an old school due to its faded brick exterior; its three levels; and, within, its buckled flooring, plus the lingering odor of wood and a cleaning product. What distinguishes the school is a sense of order. P.S. 108 runs like a business, with adults visible and vocal in the hallways, urging students to get to class on time. Teachers focus on daily objectives and hold students accountable for listening, learning, and practicing the skills taught in their classes.

Expectations for students appear in course guides, which are sent home for parents' review. However, teachers are careful to specify a daily class goal before each day's lesson. It took time to establish a businesslike, purposeful school climate, with students involved in learning; however, students were offered no alternative other than transferring out to another school. A daily outline of material for the day, or a worksheet, is usually visible on students' desks.

Classrooms usually come to order quickly, and students cooperate throughout their classes because they want the rewards: field trips; free time in the gym during their daily study period; access to a computer room, the library, or a space exploration lab; or working on mathematics puzzles and challenging problems along with a math teacher, or aiding a teacher with a specialty in geological studies. Instructors agree to offer special projects and learning units in their own areas of interest.

The building's adults set high expectations for students, both in and outside of classes. Students adapt to learning the curriculum and achieving because there seems no alternative. Students who are rewarded with special projects and explorations in their areas of interest seem to learn more in classes. Students who do not like the school and its program may transfer to other middle schools. There have been eight transfers out in the last four years.

Is this type of educational environment good for all students? What alternatives outside of classroom work might also be included, in your opinion? Do students need rewards for learning?

THE LEARNING ATMOSPHERE

Instructors from P.S. 108 pinpoint the factors that seem to encourage learning, as well as more positive attitudes toward school. They have created this list of factors:

1. A down-to-business, on-task approach during every class, every day
2. Clear objectives for each course, plus expectations for students' mastery of objectives
3. Objectives taught in each class, with appropriate review and re-teaching, as needed
4. Tutorials (one-on-one instruction or groups of three students with a teacher)
5. Acknowledgment and rewards for academic mastery and achievement on tests, plus a variety of assessments: projects; test scores; essays or question-and-answer tests
6. Spelling and vocabulary units, with in-class study/review and testing

7. Frequent communication with parents regarding students' progress
8. Extra review classes are taught, some in single-student-and-teacher sessions, as needed; topics include how to study specific subjects; preparing to write an essay—the five fundamentals; effective note-taking; spelling/vocabulary review tailored to grade level; review of the vocabulary of mathematics, geometry, and algebra (creating interest for current mastery of math, plus future learning); review of literary terms (*plot; theme; point of view*, etc.); keys to success in social studies readings—what to look for in each chapter; mastery of word problems; understanding formulas; reviewing and application of ratios and equations
9. Assessment and review of effective organizational strategies before writing an exam answer or essay or single-page inquiry about a subject (for example, What news story is prominent right now and why is our understanding of it important? Student and teacher evolve the organization of a sample essay answer)
10. Outlining: mastery of constructing a sample outline on a familiar topic and follow-up practice of the skill
11. Essentials of studying and reviewing course work for each subject on a daily basis, plus reviewing strategies for tests.

READINESS

1. What is an appropriate atmosphere for academic success?
2. In your experience, do students succeed more readily in learning through hands-on projects rather than through practicing specific skills? For example, some students learn spelling by writing out each word a number of times. Are you aware of factual data showing that a variety of methods are best? Identify a variety of methods (e.g., rote learning; associating the unknown new concept with a previously learned concept connected to the subject), plus specific techniques that engage students in the learning process.

3. What do yearly standardized test scores reveal about students' learning? Do the tests cover both types of learning (experiential and skills-based learning)?
4. How might instructors utilize a basic skills approach so that students would achieve command of a variety of skills, including hands-on learning and reading from a textbook? What experiences might you share in favor of one or the other approach, in addition to supplementary experiences (viewing a movie about a subject, followed by discussion, for example)?

RESPONSIBILITY

1. Teachers will invariably tailor lessons to a variety of students' learning styles, but how does an instructor accommodate all students' learning styles? Some students learn via projects, others through the textbook, still others with applications of problem-solving.
2. What is the role of ongoing assessment of students' progress? Can students adapt, and master the objectives set for each grade level, with a variety of approaches? What observations from your experience reveal that students learn using a variety of methods? What makes ongoing communication with parents of students possible, in view of instructors' limited free time? It seems that contacts with parents invariably lead to student improvements.

RESPONSE

1. Teachers are usually open to trying new approaches. Is this true of alternating a number of styles of learning (e.g., book-learning, completing projects, computer applications)?
2. What student success rate might indicate that a variety of styles with specific units is appropriate? In your own experience, which methods taught students successfully?

3

AN ADMINISTRATOR'S STYLE

The leadership review committee of Midlands United School District meets to consider the process of searching for and selecting a new high school principal. All committee members are to some extent overwhelmed with the task before them. Dr. Shapiro has stated that their judgment will influence the experiences of faculty, students, and staff throughout the person's tenure. He cautions fellow committee members to proceed deliberately, but perhaps, slowly.

The five committee members include Darryl Manning, Boyd Chalmers, Ann Peterson, Charles Shapiro, and Aviva Turner. Manning and Shapiro want to pinpoint an approach to use, such as a leadership model, and Chalmers and Turner mention setting up criteria, perhaps a candidate's experience and style, to utilize in deciding whom to invite to the district. They will make recommendations, taking into consideration the double-duty job: in this district, the experienced principal they hire will also mentor and advise the middle school leader, who is new to school leadership. However, they also realize the lead administrator of the high school may best be "a go-getter-type of person," according to Turner.

Peterson advises her peers, who feel the retiring principal, Dr. Richter, was "one in a million" among school leaders, "You can't replace Dr. Richter. Instead, we might look for the qualities that make a leader effective in the nuts and bolts of the job, but also effective with students—if those are our priorities." She also suggests the committee create a list of desirable qualities, including personality traits and approach or style of leading. All committee members seem relieved that they have a starting point. "I am open to any qualified individual who wants to assume the challenge," notes Chalmers. "It's just not an easy job, as I see it."

Manning volunteers to take notes on a list of committee members' preferences in terms of the potential new leader's approach and involvement in issues affecting students. Turner wonders about how much experience they might expect from a candidate, and several other committee members urge everyone to wait and see, giving each candidate a chance to review his or her relevant background and experiences, rather than make a hasty judgment regarding any specific requirement.

Although there is no theme or specific order to the list, the qualities, skills, and preferences listed are thought-provoking, as well as being on-target for the position. The consensus seems to be that the ideal candidate would maintain high visibility: visiting classes; spending at least one-half to two-thirds of his or her time walking throughout the senior high building; appearing in the cafeteria during lunch times; and remaining available to anyone—student or adult—with a question or problem to share. The new leader would be visible at athletic events and student productions, if possible.

Manning continues the list with "he or she should be a shirt-sleeves kind of leader," and others in succession add the following: "open"; "informal"; "if a male, he always wears a tie, though his coat may be in his office"; "the principal shows a formality in public"; "he or she has a good sense of humor"; "strives to be judiciously fair"; "engages in 'ordinary conversation,' such as 'How is your day going so far?'"; "espouses specific expectations for students' behavior and academic work"; "enjoys the job"; "gets to know as many students as possible and is always willing to schedule time for anyone who wants to see him"; "the leader never raises his voice with students" and "could be the ideal counselor type of person—calm, collected, unruffled"; "laughs easily"; "is approachable, plus positive and optimistic"; "wants to try new approaches or strategies for eliciting the best academic efforts from each student"; "is honest, sincere and knows how to tell a student to 'straighten up' in terms of a young adult's behavior so that he gains compliance." There is silence, followed by Turner's perception that "also, he is an authority, but doesn't throw his authority around or try to intimidate anyone."

Shapiro offers a few more ideas to conclude their list: the principal-elect is a forceful presence and also a good listener; offers feedback, whether about sports, academics, or other issues; clearly identifies what appropriate behavior is; and praises—and encourages—young people's good behavior and also gives them a second chance, if warranted.

The job goals mentioned by the committee members include the following: facilitates the smooth running of the school (and the junior high, if the new administrator wants feedback); expects students to know the school rules and procedures; approaches every problem looking for a solution that takes into account all those affected by the problem and its solution; enjoys interactions with students; and prioritizes the academic program and teachers' requests so they may do their jobs well. The new administrator must also praise and encourage efforts of faculty, staff, and students.

4

AUTHORITATIVE
INSTRUCTORS

CASE STUDY 1

Ada Summers teaches middle schoolers, maintaining a no-nonsense attitude and making it clear she is the boss in her social studies class. Students must conform to her procedures and expectations. Some students cannot finish the in-class assignments she collects and grades. Their understanding is that they will receive a lower grade if they do not finish a worksheet.

Summers is a fixture at Eugene Field Middle School. She is ageless, and unlikely to yield to group work ("an opportunity to talk or socialize" in her view) or films. She advises, "Let's train students in reference work—finding information that is up-to-date on the computer" and "precision work." By the latter she means specific answers, not "filler."

Summers prefers instilling a sense of responsibility in all students and a sense of timely work: get to work immediately, identify the task or question you need to address, do not waste any class time, provide page references to the text or reference, and do not confer with other students.

Her method is "unfriendly," as one student labeled it, and requests for class changes occur, usually during the first two weeks of school. Dr. Don Hebert, the principal, makes the calls to students' homes, explaining that all classes are filled, that Summers is highly regarded, and that students learn the entire curriculum with her. She is seasoned, knowledgeable, and professional, and so Hebert suggests that an "adjustment" may be called for on the part of students.

Not all parents—let alone their children—are pleased to hear that class changes are not possible.

"How can students learn if they are nervous, anxious?" Jean Harris asks. Harris feels she and other parents may address the board members at their next meeting. If a class change is not possible, then she might well homeschool her son or enroll him in a private school.

A number of parents have talked about their concerns and about Summers' methods; they want their children to enjoy learning, and enjoy their teachers. They don't expect teachers to entertain, but they do expect their children's personalities and styles of learning to be respected, if not accommodated. "Darryl's education is the most important thing in the world to me," explains Karen Traynor. "However, there has to be give-and-take. It's as though social studies class operates with a teacher who is not pleasant. The district board needs to know about the situation."

Some students dread social studies class because of Summers. They seem genuinely anxious and upset, as though they are defeated when they enter her room. Is a good education possible in this kind of classroom? How can we be sure Summers accommodates students who work at a careful yet slower pace than other students?

Consider the following:

1. Are middle school students likely to suffer harm from a forceful, demanding instructor? Summers expects students to adapt to her requirements. Her class sizes range from 21 to 23 students.

2. Compare and contrast Summers' approach to your teachers in grades 6–8. Was there a disciplinarian among your instructors? Think about the bosses whom you have worked with. Also, consider some of the more distant college and university professors. Might Summers actually help prepare students for high school and beyond?

3. Do students learn more or learn better in a relaxed classroom atmosphere? Some elementary teachers, for example, dress up to portray book characters and share their points of view with the classes reading the assigned books. Students are enthralled.

4. How might you explain to students that the opportunity to learn the objectives for their grade level with Mrs. Summers is a good thing? It may be a tough sell, though worth the time it takes to talk with students. They might not have heard about teachers who have a type of personality to which they are not accustomed.

5. If you were Hebert, might you confer with Summers and inform her about the sensitivity of her students, which might influence their learning in her class? Is there a history of this type of behavior from students who are uncomfortable with her?

The no-nonsense instructor seems distant, even remote, from her students. Despite years of classroom experience and a good command of teaching strategies and the curriculum, plus excellent knowledge of social studies, Summers is not a "people person."

With the desire for order during the class that this teacher insists on, can any group of seventh- and eighth-graders meet her expectations? Even group work, in this professional's opinion, must be orderly, and students must be seen but not heard.

In addition, students think they spend too little class time online, especially since there is computer access for each student. Pupils' frank comments include "She's too hard" and "Class is boring," as well as "She never smiles."

Is it possible that students will not learn as much from an authoritarian-style instructor as they might with a congenial, knowledgeable professional who enjoys teaching and also loves the subject? Will her students, in fact, dislike social studies as a result of this teacher?

CASE STUDY 2

Dr. Craig Matthews values the rigor and discipline accompanying the study of mathematics and the sciences. He teaches two calculus classes this semester at the high school and is, as usual, pleased with the students' interest.

There have been no complaints about the worksheets and outlines he distributes in each class. Students use a binder and create their own study guides with the daily handouts. Some would call his class old-fashioned and/or dull. But Matthews has set the unvarying format for this class, and he sticks to the fundamentals.

His students seem to accept his daily reviews, drills, and even quizzes, in addition to the worksheets. No student wants to drop his class after three weeks of school; he has received no parent calls or complaints. He cannot recall any parent calling him with concerns about academic rigor since he began teaching.

Summary

Matthews' personality and teaching style are low-key; many students would term his class "boring." Is the value of the class diminished and his extensive knowledge in the subject wasted if he creates a dull class?

When two visitors from the Far East observed Matthews' class, one fell asleep. As a result, this teacher and his students lowered their voices, and the lesson proceeded to the end.

Although he uses the board or overhead projector to write out terms, set up problems and solutions, and provide additional examples, he seems to keep a very fast pace in classes. Students must read the chapters thoroughly and work out example problems in advance of class meetings in order to keep up with Matthews.

If there were relevant films available, this instructor might show them, but that is not the case: "There are none," he says. Computer applications are few and far between, except for the yearly meetings of advanced mathematics professors. One of his student teachers remained with Matthews for a week and a day before asking to work with Mae Gibbs instead, citing how "predictable" the calculus classes were. Would students learn more with an animated classroom leader?

Questions

1. Why does Matthews receive no complaints about the difficult subject he teaches?
2. Might other teachers use or adapt his no-nonsense approach to class sessions—or can they do so? Of what value is his style of instruction?
3. There seem to be no problems with negative student attitudes. Does this indicate that they are learning calculus?

ANOTHER STUDY, IN CONTRAST

Mr. Messner is a first-year instructor who is determined his high school classes will learn economics. When he notices a continuing problem with the sixth-period group whispering to one another and others not paying attention, he suddenly grabs the old, thick, wooden pole with a metal window-opener hook on the end, and raps it as hard as he can on his large desk to capture students' attention.

1. Is his method a good one to use to bring students back on track during a lesson?
2. What other methods might engage students in Messner's goals and the class activity for the day?

3. Messner has a short temper. Will his temper command students each time they see it?
4. What might you advise him to use as a follow-up tactic in order to avoid the noisy demonstration?

CONSIDERATIONS

1. Classes are large in many districts, averaging 21.1 students in elementary schools and 23.5 in secondary schools, according to the *Digest of Education Statistics.*
2. Students in grades K through 12 are not all highly motivated, attentive, quiet learners.
3. Students may respond well to computer instruction.
4. Some students exhibit less than ideal behaviors and attitudes.
5. Students in some classes shout out comments, disrupt instruction, and seem not to value learning; parents may not know how to encourage their children or address their academic weaknesses.
6. Objectives per grade level must be taught in all subjects.
7. Distracting teachers is a diversion from academics, which teachers must deal with.
8. Teachers control classes as best they can; if there is a routine after checking attendance and it includes homework checking, an in-class activity (a worksheet, for example), and a quiz at the end of the class, this constitutes a workable routine.
9. Teachers attend to optimizing the learning conditions, and they will continue to do so.
10. Small-group instruction and small-group work on review materials and outlines, chapter discussions, and so forth work best for a number of students.
11. There may be a place for question/answer drills based on homework assignments.
12. Practice tests reviewed before a final test seem to help most students.

13. Teachers with a good sense of humor, who utilize it in class, tend to divert classes by providing a break from homework review or drills—and this may well help students return to their class work.
14. Not all teachers have ideal personalities—nor do all bosses, all team members working on a specific project, or all individuals who share an office at work or serve together on a committee.
15. Chatty students who are friends outside of class often bring the desire to continue conversations into a class if they are all assigned to a specific section.
16. Class work is not always fun.

READINESS

1. Summers might use a letter to parents anticipating students' potential unfamiliarity with new teaching/learning strategies. She can reinforce her desire for students to grow as independent learners who are also responsible and who achieve at their highest potential.
2. School administrators know Summers' policies and may have to briefly review her classroom methods with any concerned parent who phones in to inquire.
3. Are students ready for "the bridge to high school" opportunities offered in middle school? Might this idea receive some emphasis in any number of classrooms?
4. Requiring students to be more independent learners who also work well in groups may take a year or more of experience, which is the "bridge" idea.
5. Summers expects her students to succeed academically. She provides structured, predictable classes, with students assuming some measure of the responsibility for learning. Is this an outdated concept?
6. All district instructors are encouraged by Hebert to individualize learning for students who require it.

RESPONSE

1. Summers invites parents to call and make an appointment to join the class, or to meet with her and talk during lunch break.
2. Many district teachers ask students to have an adult at home read and sign their assignment notebooks on a regular basis.
3. All teachers might assess and suggest online access of key sites related to their class units.

RESPONSIBILITY

1. The district newsletter might feature an article about the variety of teaching and learning strategies utilized by professionals in the local schools. Teachers might provide short descriptions and explanations of their favorite learning units or methods.
2. Hebert encourages his staff to utilize the library, as well as newspapers and books, in planning and approaching course objectives. He stresses their assignment of independent learning projects to students, whether reading or creating models, a scenario, or a dialogue (of characters in a book, for example), after which the students report back to other class members.
3. Summers teaches students how to complete homework assignments.

5

CHANGING STUDENT
ATTITUDES

Dr. Dennis Baker, an in-service speaker addressing the faculty and staff of Amherst Heights School District, is direct and forceful with those gathered for the opening in-service workshop of the new school year. Baker insists that it is the responsibility of all instructors to teach the attitudes and behaviors of success on a daily basis. The goal of learning, he notes, must include students' involvement, for if students are engaged in learning and involved in class activities, they are directed toward the course goals and objectives. They will succeed academically and continue practicing successful academic habits. Moreover, they will realize an enjoyable sense of pride in their achievement, which will encourage repetition of the success. All school personnel, he notes, can affect students positively by expressing interest in students and their progress per year; it is essential that the entire school community support students.

The breakout sessions are for review and discussion of effective practices and in-class activities to involve students. "Make the students accountable for their own learning," insists Baker. Individual teacher groups rejoin the large-group session to apply their discussions to current policies and practices. The topic is reviewing techniques and practices to create successful experiences that encourage students to repeat and reinforce their successes.

A listing of attitudes and habits, as well as new behaviors, emerges from the instructors' groups. Students' *success attitudes* include awareness of the importance of all subjects and all assignments; possessing a positive, open approach to all classes; maintaining a "can-do" attitude and the willingness to spend time as needed to understand each class and each homework assignment as part of a larger unit of study; experiencing a renewed or new appreciation for education as a means to additional education and, eventually, a satisfying job in a chosen career field; renewing the value of academic skill areas as a part of growth and learning; possessing the willingness to remediate academic weaknesses, if present, plus reminding oneself periodically about the importance of asking questions in class and renewing one's decision to succeed.

The list of behaviors includes paying attention in each class; having a single focus related to what the instructor wants students to know or do for each class meeting (practice a new skill, for example); asking questions; engaging in the lesson of the day and participating; joining in the review of previous lessons, reinforcing learning; utilizing quiet study time, if necessary—working alone with a math problem, for example, before discussing the steps to its solution; concentrating on one subject, one class at a time; working on one subject at a time during homework hours; and reading assignments and asking questions as the reading proceeds—for example, "What is the single idea on this page that is the most important concept?"

One reminder relates to a student's decision to succeed: the decision must be a personal commitment to utilize available time to study and review, as needed, whether at home with assigned questions to answer or problems to solve, or in class, learning and reviewing with students or teachers. Examples of a student's commitment may include involvement in each class by asking questions about a chapter or stating facts learned during the reading; or creating possible questions in a group about the importance of the unit of study or chapter, and raising the questions for others in the class to respond to. The teacher might hand out review questions, but each student assumes the responsibility for answering one or more questions in class. Class activities can vary: group work allows students to solve specific problems with the input of others; students may give individual short speeches related to review questions; and a set of problems based on application of reading assignments might be posed for group work.

Students' behavior may change when students know what is expected of them and when they receive materials such as study questions or a practice test specifically designed for their review and understanding. Students' attitudes may change, becoming more positive, when they realize the variety of methods utilized to review and study material, whether singly or in groups or panels. Their study at home provides independent work, and students may raise questions from study at home to ask in class. Experiencing success comes from involvement in a course of study; teachers plan and select activities to involve students.

READINESS

1. Teachers can compile worksheets that include explanations of and questions for all learning units. Worksheets become study guides for testing.
2. Parents help by reminding children about their commitment to do well, in terms of the goals and objectives of their courses. Sending home a unit of study for parents' signatures may keep interested adults apprised of the course of study and requirements. Instructors might review study skills in terms of each new learning unit.
3. Additional textbooks or supplementary texts may be available in the students' library for a different approach or point of view, or for a review of material.

4. Teachers can review with students how to outline a chapter, or how to isolate key ideas in a chapter and either highlight them or create a study guide for test review.
5. Instructors might exchange ideas and suggestions with other instructors to acquire new methods, unique approaches, or new readings and activities to relate to specific units, especially if these new approaches create student interest.
6. Teachers can teach the vocabulary of a subject area as terms appear in readings.

RESPONSIBILITY

1. Challenge all students with a variety of approaches to material, as well as a variety of assignments.
2. Allow students to assume responsibility for learning by participating in small-group reviews; raising questions that might appear as essay questions; and creating quizzes on specific portions of the readings.
3. Collect a variety of worksheets or exercises and exchange these with other teachers of the subject; some students will need extra review of material.
4. If a student is unwilling to complete assignments or exercises related to the units or to attend a tutorial appointment, as needed, call the parents and also alert the student's counselor, to help motivate and renew the student's commitment to the class and to learning.
5. Monitor each student's progress in mastering course goals. Share with parents, using a take-home explanation and listing of current grades. Suggest remediation, as needed, or offer praise, as needed. Feedback is essential.
6. Look for a pattern of weakness that may be common among a group of students; it may be a gap in a previous course that needs to be addressed.

RESPONSE

1. Isolate the objective(s) of each day's lesson and unit of study as you teach it.
2. Center classroom study on skills students need to know. Pinpoint these skills in specific jobs or careers.
3. Remedy students' weaknesses: Is there a learning lab for individualized help? Might department committees suggest additional learning resources for students?
4. Enlist parents' help with reminders about students' need to attain the best grades they can and a thorough knowledge of each subject. Students who learn to work diligently and consistently pave the way for their own success in higher education and in job settings.
5. Ongoing assessment of effective teaching strategies and increased student engagement might be provided for all teachers to utilize.
6. Encourage students' efforts toward mastering skills per grade level and subject. Share positive news about students' progress with parents.
7. Review study techniques, making sure students know how to study each of their subjects. Include note-taking and the use of notes for reviewing. Encourage reaching beyond the textbook to apply learning to other courses and even to potential jobs.
8. Have students read a page and then come up with one sentence about the most important idea on the page. This is good practice, applicable to most courses students take, now and later.

6

COUNSELORS AND
STUDENTS'
WELL-BEING

Newly elected board member Sherlene Hammond wants to explore the financial issues of Unified School District 125 during her first board meeting. Some of Hammond's constituents insist that the district counseling department budget is too high and may be out of control; one local business owner even used the word *extravagant* about certain departments' expenses. An editorial in the local *Herald* questioned items in various departments' budgets, urging residents to "demand to know what we are paying for." Hammond looks at the first agenda item of the evening's meeting and sighs; it is a request for three new counselors for the senior high building.

"What do counselors do each day?" she asks. "Can they give us a list of their school commitments on a typical day? How much counseling of students takes place, for example?" There is a pause before anyone addresses the questions.

Board members share their knowledge about counselors' duties. Henry Turner replies, "They meet with teachers, parents, coaches, and academic chairpersons, as needed. But I know they primarily counsel students on a variety of issues, plus schedule the next semester's classes for all their counselees, besides filling out forms and creating reports." Janice Meeks adds, "I know they have input on new programs, and they confer with the department chairs." Turner offers another responsibility: "You know, they need basic information on each counselee. That must take an awful lot of time. Plus, they have input on their students' behavior problems or on various academic issues."

Soon, Philo Cutler adds his impression: "We can't overlook a source of meaningful give-and-take between our counselors and teens who face their most critical life stages. Think about students' issues: careers; college or trade school or full-time employment; problems and the expectations of parents; the pressures of academics and sports, plus getting along with friends. I know group situations are not easy for many young people. Identity issues are troubling if not talked about. I know I couldn't handle a counselor's job. It must be exhausting."

Todd Springer recalls seeing a counselor's day-planner book, with no open spaces that day—every single slot was filled. "I don't know if I could handle that day by day," he adds. "Plus, counselors fill out profile reports on each student. Counselors are responsible for the letters of recommendation sent to the colleges students apply to."

Counselors' caseloads could not be tougher: depending on school size, counselors may be responsible for 250 students. In some districts, counselors' caseloads total 400–600 students. Counselors administer tests in most schools, plus they have administrative duties. Attending professional meetings, conferences, and conventions is also part of their time commitment. The job may be more challenging and demanding than most parents and even school personnel realize.

Consider a single student's well-being in grades 7 through 12; the questions, problems, and challenges that may bring students into counselors' offices; the troubling issues include drugs and drug sellers on campus. Alcohol and/or drugs may be available at parties, and some junior-high parents leave their homes so their children and friends feel "more comfortable" while socializing there. Additional problems students may face include bullying, both inside and outside of school. Some student cliques can be vicious to students whom the group members perceive to be unlike them. Shakedown groups extort money from students in some schools, just as gangs do. The latter make their presence and expectations known to students, whom they may attack if the students wear or show gang symbols, wear special colors and patterns, or exhibit hand signs and the like. Gang members most often do not fear administrators or students; they remain in school, waiting to quit when they reach the age of accountability.

Many students are aware of peer pressure, to excel or to join in on the "fun" of upsetting the order of school. Counselors eventually learn about some of the problems their counselees face, and yet the negative experiences remain with young people, sometimes throughout their lives.

Most students visit counselors as they fill out applications for higher education; usually, students ask for help in writing the application's essay, which typically asks, "Why do you want to attend State Tech (or some other institution)?" Presenting themselves on paper is not easy for most students. Other issues also challenge students, who may turn to counselors for help. These issues include awareness of cheating on tests; the pressure of team sports; the problem of choosing a branch of service instead of college, or postponing schooling for a while; the use of tobacco or drugs; penalties for violating school rules; and peer pressure.

Dropping out of school may seem like a good idea at times, and many youths think about it. Also, some young adults deal with an unplanned pregnancy or a friend's alcohol use, or depression, confusion, uncertainty, or identity issues. Counselors also see special needs students and often are a lifeline for them, helping them with issues of adjustment and class requirements; these students may require more time than other students. In addition, the number of nonnative students in some schools, particularly in large urban areas, grows larger year by year. Some of these students' parents do not speak English, and counselors serve the role of an adult model in what may be a difficult setting for some students.

Currently, counselors must get to know students in terms of another chilling reality: some students plot—sometimes with accomplices of similar mindsets—major disruptions of learning, or make plans to threaten students and school personnel. They may carry weapons or have access to guns.

Counselors watch out for student attitudes and behaviors that may indicate that a counselee needs an intervention before he or she takes disruptive action. Some potential hints of problems may appear in a student's anger or silent brooding; a resentment of what he or she perceives as laws and rules handed down, that he or she must follow; a persistent unhappiness; or an inappropriate sense of humor at others' expense. The student who plots mayhem often resents school, finding classes and requirements restrictive and unnecessary. That individual may need help but not see the consequences of his or her actions, even the consequences of disruptive or potentially harmful events. The student may be reckless; setting fires in trash cans, for example, "for fun," may fulfill a desire to upset the order and stability of a school system that is in place and operating well. A school might seem a perfect target for "shaking up": some students regard an orderly school as a dare, or an invitation to see what they can do to disrupt it.

Counselors can help students with the issues that challenge them, many of which are listed, but counselees also exhibit depression and anxiety or even behavioral problems; some are unaware of the causes, not recognizing that there is disorder in their lives or their thinking. How much time counselors can give to large caseloads becomes an issue at pivotal periods in students' lives. Whatever the counselor/student ratio might be, counselors by training have the ability and interest to facilitate a young adult's school experience. Are the numbers of counselees too many to facilitate each student's school experience, year by year? What can we do to change that reality in schools where it is the norm?

READINESS

1. School district leaders might suggest a review of the current school budget in terms of adding additional qualified, competent counselors. Counselors are a critical resource for a large number of students with a variety of issues, including scheduling.
2. Might school counselors be relieved of administrative duties? These can include hall monitoring, cafeteria or study hall supervision, proctoring tests, and other assignments.
3. Attending conferences and conventions allows counselors to learn about new services and new approaches to student problems, as well as giving them the opportunity to review successful day-to-day procedures and practices. Exchanges with other professionals can be beneficial for both counselors and their students. Do the counselors in schools you know of attend professional meetings and conventions, reporting back to other members of their department?
4. A school or district psychologist may be a worthwhile addition to the faculty and staff, in view of a contemporary youth population whose members face a wide range of potential problems.
5. If a student is not succeeding in classes, how might a counselor intervene? What examples can you offer of successful interventions that you are aware of?
6. How do counselors encourage parents and/or other trusted adults in the home to monitor and guide a student's progress in school and his social *comfort* (for lack of a better term)? A counselor's article in the district newsletter on this topic, with specific ideas and techniques parents might not have considered, may be helpful.
7. How might a "crisis" phone number operate for students? Might counselors or other school adults be available to deal with students' questions and problems, whether academic or personal issues?

RESPONSIBILITY

1. Each student counselee has unique problems, and counselors ideally facilitate students' successful progress through grade 12. What changes in counselors' caseloads, schedules, and effective policies and practices might allow a counselor to give adequate time to all the students who comprise his or her caseload?

2. What alternative school professionals might become resource individuals for students? Is it possible for each school's administrators to ask school adults to serve students in this way, especially in view of counselors' caseloads?

3. How do we emphasize each student's abilities, interests, and skills as a basis not only for course selections, but also for additional training and educational opportunities after graduation? How do we single out available internships and scholarships, plus local employers and other business leaders who might help specific students toward a career, or toward success in the workplace?

4. How might we encourage students' academic progress? Are there math labs, for example, in a school with which you are familiar? How about a study center—to help students review effective skills and techniques for specific courses?

5. Do school professionals offer students adequate information about local junior colleges, colleges, universities, trade schools, and vocational services, and about testing opportunities for students to highlight their skills and interests? How do we steer students toward exploring the availability of training and learning after graduation?

RESPONSE

1. Might counselors meet with all counselees more than once per year? With large caseloads, how might these *additional* meetings occur?

2. Encouraging all students to join school clubs and groups related to their interests, or community groups offering socializing and activities in specific areas—such as coin-collecting clubs, Scouting organizations, theater groups, or second-language conversation groups—is also a worthwhile goal for counselors and a good investment of students' time. Might another school professional guide students specifically to such opportunities in surrounding communities?

3. Counselors might call homes and review select counselees' academic progress in classes, as well as reviewing the opportunities that are available for additional tutoring or supplemental instruction with teachers.

4. Confer with fellow counselors about how they might handle unusual student problems and move toward solutions. These might include social isolation; failing a gym class; or a pervasive dislike of school and inability to function in classes. Have you encountered any students in these situations?

5. Teaching students how to research colleges and post-high-school training in their fields of interest is also important to their futures; who else might know sources of interest for many students?

6. Create a study skills seminar to reteach students how to study, how to read and take notes on units of study, and successful methods of test taking.

7. Invite local college and university representatives to speak to students during lunch hours or in an assembly, for example, to explain their schools' offerings, internships, summer courses, scholarships, and applications for financial aid assistance.

7

CREATING AND SUSTAINING PARENTAL PARTNERSHIPS

The city of Fort Washington changed when Burrell Wilson inherited his father's mill; the new CEO tied the future success of the business to relocating operations. Wilson thought about the Great Lakes area, preferred for its access to airports, interstate highways, and nearby services and industries. He knew he could tailor a state-of-the-art mill to current trends in the industry. Wilson Sr. retired, to allow his son to run the business as he chose.

The new CEO asked all employees to consider relocating with him to the Midwest; in fact, he welcomed their expertise and ideas. Some embraced the chance, while the majority chose not to move. Changes in the area occurred, more quickly than anticipated. The big mill, emptied, did not draw any interested buyers. Within months of the mill's closing, several restaurants near the business closed or relocated. Moreover, a population shift occurred as former mill workers moved on to other jobs, and new residents who could suddenly afford more reasonable housing rates took advantage of the availability of many devalued properties. Then a department store closed, followed by some specialty stores and one major multi-purpose big-box store.

The Fort Washington United School District 113 student population also changed. A new, pressing issue involved the specific skills on state-mandated testing. Results showed 34 percent of district 113 students through grade 12 tested below the average yearly progress expected for their grades. Department meetings and in-service sessions revealed teachers' concerns about students' weak preparation for their current instructional objectives. Faculty members agreed that remediation and improved test results were necessary.

Of great interest, however, was the fact that most district school administrators, support staff, and faculty targeted one important factor as a cause of concern. Research seemed to suggest that parents' and other significant adults' involvement in K–12 students' academic endeavors led to higher grades overall. Might weak academic skills and students not achieving at grade-level expectations also tie in with the lower state-test scores?

The topic of most concern to administrators and faculty members became a question: How do we engage and maintain parents' interest and involvement in their children's academic efforts, especially in grades 6 through 12? Dr. Macon, the district superintendent, suggested that instructors start a dialogue, joining specific discussion groups comprising school administrators, department chairs, and instructors, meeting on a regular basis to review perceived problems and available remediation efforts and highlight how to engage parents as partners in their children's success.

READINESS

1. Students understand they have the responsibility to participate in efforts to relearn material, to achieve well in classes, and to perform on tests showing mastery of grade-level objectives.

2. Teachers review objectives per course and grade level with students, and identify and utilize available resources, including one-on-one work with tutors, as needed.
3. Group review in all classes and subject areas will allow students to progress toward mastery of essential skills and knowledge of the concepts necessary to move on to new objectives and, eventually, the next grade.
4. Review of study skills occurs in all classes, as does identification of at-home preparation for the next day's classes.
5. Administrators publicize the new program's goal namely to bring students up to their grade levels. Community members with specific skills and specialties tied to the schools' objectives are encouraged to tutor. Other adults are encouraged to provide rides to school for students' tutoring sessions.
6. Administrators use counselor feedback about the program and students' efforts toward remediation.

RESPONSIBILITY

1. School district personnel, especially classroom instructors, play key roles in the academic gains of all their students, especially those who need remediation. Private tutors may also have a place in remediation and new learning.
2. Parents understand the assessment criteria and the tutorial programs that are necessary for their children to succeed in each subject area. They reveal their interest and involvement in their children's learning. They also understand that remediation and review of essential skills are keys to academic success.
3. Community members, tutors, and former instructors with specific skills in the required grade-level objectives volunteer as supplemental support personnel and/or tutors. These local residents may motivate students to succeed.
4. The new review and relearning program aimed toward students' achievement and mastery of objectives for their grade

levels is publicized. Publicity will draw more interested adults to become involved in changing students' outlook regarding academics, as well as in helping students master learning objectives in all their classes.

RESPONSE

1. Isolate specific, grade-level skills which reveal individual students' weaknesses.
2. Make sure that skills work, remediation, and one-on-one tutoring or small learning groups (three to five students) are ongoing, weekly efforts.
3. Encourage students to change any negative perceptions or attitudes toward specific subjects, teachers, classes, or remediation efforts, and facilitate these changes.
4. Review with students the need to achieve academic goals in order to advance to the next grade and in order to graduate.
5. Instructors, be sure to encourage students' specific efforts and progress—every day, if possible.

SUPPLEMENTAL STEPS SUGGESTED BY DISCUSSION GROUPS OF FACULTY, STAFF, AND ADMINISTRATORS

1. Publicize the program [Tutorial to Mastery program: Catch Up and Succeed]. Use local newspaper coverage to explain the program, as well as local news television. The superintendent or principal may run spots to explain the program and encourage community adults to help, if desired. The theme is "Students' Learning: Our Students' Academic Success Is Their Future," or "We Can Give Our Students Their Chance to Succeed in the World, in Higher Education, in Jobs and Careers."
2. Engage community college specialists for tutoring, as needed; enlist former district instructors, adult volunteers, religious

leaders, and members with academic skills in major subject areas to tutor one-on-one or to provide rides, as needed, to and from sessions.

3. Show interest in students daily, in classes and during activities, and convey encouragement for individual efforts. This applies to all school personnel.

4. Help students attend tutorials, as needed.

5. Create a security force of adults with experience to monitor buildings and grounds during tutorials.

6. Arrange meetings with a parent, or another significant adult in the student's life, and a school counselor; maintain a dialogue with this adult; contact about progress and concerns, milestones met, achievements, and so forth.

7. Set up Saturday morning school for review, catch-up, and skills practice. (Some students may have difficulty with more than one subject.)

8. Establish regular, weekly contact with a parent or a significant adult in the student's life to give progress reports, share concerns, accept suggestions, and get feedback.

9. Print an illustrative flyer or brochure about the program. Seek funds to disseminate printed flyers that explain the philosophy of academic success.

10. Utilizing a counselor team, evolve a student-readiness profile for incoming high school freshmen, to be used in the district eighth grades. Have a counselor team visit junior high schools for talks with students (in assemblies), to review the program.

11. Emphasize the partnership between the school district and the individual's home using weekly calls; open-house hours at school and/or on Saturday; and input from school psychologists. Create a readiness assessment for middle school students viewing high school in their future. Enlist the help of behaviorists or psychologists to review personality profiles and stages in development toward increased maturity. Newsletters might feature students and activities, progress, and suggestions for parents' input and help, as well as emphasizing the importance of skills learning.

SCHOOL LEADER FOCUS

1. What steps are likely indicated to draw agreement and support regarding tutorials and supplemental study to achieve grade-level mastery? Is it a public relations issue?
2. How do schools sell the need for reteaching toward mastery? How do we enlist the cooperation and support of students who need the extra help? How do we inform parents and students about the bridge between high school and future jobs?
3. What channels of communication have proven effective, in your experience, for enlisting community support and parents' understanding of the school's program and objectives?
4. How can local athletes and successful graduates encourage and educate students who need extra help?
5. Is Saturday school an option, say from 9:00 A.M. until noon?

8

DISAFFECTED
STUDENTS

Depression is a psychological disorder, usually a long-term disorder, and an emotionally intense condition, with a range of symptoms. Only medical professionals can diagnose an individual, and yet some students may exhibit behaviors and/or attitudes seemingly associated with a diagnosis of depression.

Some students may not feel they belong in school, even in the elementary grades; they may be estranged, out of place, in group situations. School subjects and academic activities may fail to command the interest of these students on a day-by-day basis, but that could easily apply to a number of students. However, there may have been an event or circumstance that caused a student to feel challenged or frightened or upset to the extent that the pupil does not want to return to school.

Examples follow about two students who may exhibit estrangement from school and school activities. The first is a girl who is new to the suburb she lives in; it is a prosperous community of old wealth, quite the reverse of what she has known for the first eleven years of her life. Her family has moved from one of the largest cities in the East to the Midwest.

43

Patty is overwhelmed almost immediately and feels out of place in the new school. She knows she doesn't belong. Fellow students are noticeably wealthy and privileged. Her class comprises four or five cliques of female students who have known one another for years. She does not fit in with any of these groups. The majority of class members take private lessons weekly in music, dance, gymnastics, or other specialties. They also dress very well, as though someone co-ordinates outfits for them each day. Patty is unfamiliar with private lessons; of all the students she knew in the East, she can recall none who took private lessons in sports or other pastimes.

Although there are clubs at school, the new student goes home as soon as the bell rings; she can hardly wait to leave school. It is un-comfortable for her. Peers take vacations on holidays. Both of Patty's parents work; she has never experienced a vacation.

Shy and sensitive, she remains uncomfortable in group settings. "No one is interested in being my friend," she claims. Her perception is that she does not measure up. She is certain she does not belong in this school or in the trendy, affluent suburb she now lives in.

Is this student's problem a school administrator's problem? It is if the student dislikes the school and cannot achieve at her highest academic level. The burden she faces every day is that she cannot compete with these students in any way—academically or socially. One could easily use the term *estranged* when speaking of Patty's feelings about the school environment.

A second example concerns Paul.

Although he is sixty-two years of age, Paul has never held a job, part-time or full-time, with the exception of working at his father's store during summers while he was growing up and in school. With several siblings who work in a variety of challenging fields, Paul is the exception. Each sibling has progressed to a fairly high level of professional achievement. Paul has been at home since his high school graduation and one job interview, only days after graduation.

At age eighteen he had an appointment to meet with a potential employer. Certain that he would qualify for the entry-level position as a sales associate, he looked forward to the meeting with the personnel manager. He was sure he had a very good chance of starting the job as soon as they wanted him.

The interview questions were standard: What is your experience in sales? Why should we hire you? We will interview a number of applicants—why should we select you as our new associate? What do you know about our store, its image, and its priorities?

Paul knew the answers to all the questions as they were posed. He began the interview by explaining why he was already a good salesman, telling the interviewer about his summers in his father's store. He didn't explain that his father, an alcoholic, provided a very good income but was distant and disgruntled, and that he tended to be mean when he drank too much. He terrified Paul at times. But both his parents insisted on all the children getting a good, sound education.

His parents made sacrifices, and his mother also began working in the family store so she and her husband would not have to hire an employee. Their sacrifices would allow them to send their children to a good private boys' school affiliated with a church. The teachers, mostly religious males, were strict disciplinarians; theirs was a rigid dogmatism about religion, and they maintained a distance from the students.

These unyielding individuals frightened Paul; but he felt there was something wrong with him when he complained to other students. They told him to "toughen up" and "take it till you graduate." Paul knew how proud his parents were of their sacrifices for him to attend the prestigious school. He endured humiliations and punishments from the teachers who wielded power and taunted students as they desired. In addition, they seemed to know Paul's weaknesses and sensitivity, using them against him. Had they talked with his father? he wondered.

When his interview began for the sales job, he explained why he was already a good salesman; he told the interviewer about his summers in his father's store. But after the questions had been posed, the interviewer unexpectedly critiqued him and his answers. "You talk too loudly and you're excited and nervous. We don't want a loud salesman. This is a classy business." There was a pause. Paul, shocked, felt he had shown his enthusiasm for the job.

But the interviewer continued. "You are too caught up in yourself. We don't have to hire you; I'm interviewing a dozen others. I get calls every day on our ad. And you gesture too much! You look around and you act nervous. No, we're not hiring you. You can leave now." The interviewer took what appeared to be Paul's application and tore it up; then he threw it in a nearby wastebasket. "You can leave now," he reminded Paul.

Paul returned home but was too ashamed to mention anything about the interview. His family members noticed his discomfort and did not question him. Paul was then frozen in time, reliving the trauma. His working career ended that day. He remains home every day, reading the newspaper, watching television, and, in the spring and summer, doing some gardening in the front and back yards.

READINESS

1. Have you participated in a meeting, briefing, or in-service session about students with what seem to be emotional problems or issues related to school? What has been your experience with those who might be disaffected in some aspect(s)? What behaviors did you notice in these students? What advice did a counselor or workshop leader offer about students with issues like those described?

2. What other characteristics of students who are emotionally traumatized, as Paul seems to have been, have you seen or known of?

3. How serious, in your opinion, is the problem of lack of connection to school, and what can be done to help students who seem very sensitive, though trusting, and who seem helpless to overcome challenging obstacles and/or possible past mistreatment or abuse?

4. How do you inform school staff members about a student who concerns you? Do you feel that a workshop or conference op-

portunity for social workers or psychologists to offer their views about students' potential psychological problems might yield insights and be productive? Have you read any articles or research related to students with issues similar to Patty's or Paul's?

RESPONSIBILITY

1. Are teachers and counselors obligated to report on and follow up with students who seem to have problems, such as what appears to be social isolation or, on the other hand, boisterous classroom behavior or extreme sensitivity to rejection?

2. What specialists are available in school districts with which you are familiar to assess and help students who seem to stand out with what may be emotional issues, or who exhibit disruptive outbursts or other unusual behaviors in class? Specialists may offer valuable suggestions to classroom teachers as well as administrators and physical education (PE) teachers. PE teachers may teach a class with one or more students who do not want to participate in the activities as required. How do we teach all students to respect and empathize with students who have behavioral issues or feelings of discomfort that surface in classes?

3. What advice might you give teachers about responding to students who exhibit inappropriate classroom behavior, who are disruptive, or who seem unusually reticent or fearful?

4. The key words for school adults who deal with potentially disaffected students may be *acknowledge, encourage,* and *support* (students and their efforts). What other advice would you offer teachers of these particular students?

RESPONSE

1. "No one likes you—are you aware that no one likes you?" Under what circumstances might a teacher use this type of "reality

check," as the instructor explained it, to respond to a student who cannot seem to pay attention in class? He frequently shouts out his opinions, disrupting others.

2. A sense of belonging in their classes seems important for some students who may never have felt at ease with a teacher or other students. How do teachers best establish an atmosphere of acceptance for all students in their classes?

3. What class activities may help students feel they are *in the right place*? How might teachers lead or instruct all students to be empathic in view of other students' behaviors, beliefs, and even their problems, as well as their opinions and questions?

4. Have you witnessed behaviors of students who may be among the disaffected? What were the behaviors exhibited, and how did you respond to the students? Did you confer with a counselor or school social worker or psychologist?

5. Teachers may observe students, listen to them, and respond to them, as well as teaching the curriculum. If a teacher takes time to point out each student's strengths, abilities, skills, and talents, that professional may have helped a student more than he or she realizes.

9

DISENGAGED STUDENTS

The term *disengaged* is used in psychology, and may comprise only one of a patient's core issues. However, some students have been labeled *disengaged*: these students lack the expected and usual attachment most other students feel toward the schools they attend. In contrast with the disengaged, think of the majority of students who pay close attention to their school's athletic teams. These students may also participate in and enjoy one or more of the school clubs and activities.

Students engaged in school cheer for their school's teams, and eagerly review with like-minded friends every good play they see on the field or court. Unlike the disengaged students, most students are proud of their school and, usually, its good reputation. In contrast, a disengaged student is emotionally separated, removed from the school he or she attends; and neutral, if not critical or sarcastic, about his or her school's teams and clubs, in addition to the school procedures and routine, and also about other students, especially if the latter participate in school activities.

Think about the publicity associated with students who bring weapons into school buildings or who plot the destruction of property or even plan to take others' lives. These may be some of the disengaged students who may not blend well with most other students. The disengaged view students who participate in school activities, who strive to achieve academically, and who enjoy the friendships a school experience allows as "followers."

The disengaged may associate with a circle of like-minded students who dislike school rules and procedures. They may express the desire to "shake things up" or "make a statement" to the school community they dislike, or to draw attention to themselves or to a political cause.

"I'll show them" may be prominent in their thinking.

A well-publicized "trench-coat group" meticulously planned the destruction of their school several years ago, including harming anyone in their path. They might have succeeded had they not drawn suspicion to themselves with the large amounts of stockpiled weapons and ammunition discovered hidden inside their homes. Disengaged students usually have good intellectual abilities, and their parents are shocked to learn that their children may have been implicated in plans to destroy property or take others' lives.

Two profiles of potential disengaged students follow.

Jay Godfrey's motivation is "Just to shake them up."

Terry O'Donnell, Jay Godfrey, and Marquis Torrence start the year and choose cafeteria seats at the same place, a table near one of the exits. At first they simply eat by themselves, though they glance briefly at their tablemates. It doesn't take much time for Terry and Jay to compliment Marquis on his unusual athletic ability. No one can overlook the talented athlete, who is very nearly as skilled as a college player. One sports reporter has described him as "a natural" on the football field, where "he comes alive."

Marquis, who automatically knows a play or instinctively responds on the field as though reading a player's manual, has never considered his athletic ability a skill; instead, he is more aware of his academic difficulties. He has trouble reading and is terribly embarrassed about it. Many students admire his athletic skill but do not know how to approach the athlete, who is considered "standoffish," and so they leave him to himself.

These three students continue to sit at the same table, and almost surprise themselves by talking and getting to know one another after several weeks. But all three are careful to keep conversations on neutral subjects, mostly complaints about their classes and teachers, the rules, and the lack of excitement in school. Soon, they become accustomed to one another.

One lunch period they talk about a San Mirinda high school that has been the subject of news reports: a small group of students held a class of students in a classroom as hostages. The perpetrator entered the classroom at a prearranged time "to show them who's the boss." When a SWAT team arrived, the experienced force easily disarmed the unsuspecting students and transported them to the police station. No one was hurt; the plotters were in custody.

"I wish that dude had thought of our beloved Hillside High first," begins Jay, leading the conversation.

"That's a very good school they held up. Nothing like that has ever happened here," reflects Terry. "Probably won't, either, with Bando [a nickname for the administrator of school security, Mr. Ronald Bandocarini] around."

"He'd be off the team, I guarantee," Marquis reminds them. Note that this athlete seems to value his sport and, in all probability, his team members. "Besides, you can't get away with anything here."

"But look at the impact!" Jay reminds both of his new acquaintances. There is a pause and then he continues, though a little hesitantly, "You think it would work here? Could we shake up the conformists and scare everyone? Is it worth a try—just for fun? Can we do it together?"

When Jay gets no response because Terry and Marquis seem to be thinking about what he has said, Jay adds the question, "What have you got to lose?"

Terry has always dreamed of testing and designing aircraft engines, hopefully in the army. Few others know he wants to enter the service. "Well, what have you guys got to lose?" repeats Jay. Terry's response is quick, surprising him. "I'm going to be an army test pilot. Hate to throw that away. My uncle was career army." The future airman surprises and silences Jay, but then Marquis follows the response with "Football." He doesn't have to say anything else.

The buzzer rings for the close of this lunch period and all three rise, moving off in three different directions. Terry and Marquis do not glance again in Jay's direction; if anything, they seem embarrassed.

READINESS

1. What response might we expect of a school security team if three students, for example, entered a classroom and took over? I assume every teacher may be able to contact security by a prearranged signal or warning of a suspicious or dangerous situation in a classroom. Review what that signal is, in your experience. Is it a good idea to leave responses to the experts in hostage attempts or "take over the class" situations?

2. What should an instructor say or do, or avoid saying or doing, in a situation of this type? Might teachers and students role-play their responses or actions in advance of an event such as that described in item 1?

3. Should a school security officer or policeman visit individual classes, or present a review of effective measures in crisis events, at the beginning of each school year, to explain the roles of both teacher and students? Do all students know how to handle such emergencies? How do the schools you know of explain and/or illustrate effective behavior in unexpected crisis situations? Is an explanation of how to react in a school crisis a part of the student handbook, for example? Do students role-play emergencies and/or practice in advance, and know the steps to take and the steps to avoid?

4. No two hostage-takers are the same. Some are determined to speak about an issue to a captive audience; others want to hold a group in power; and still others want to frighten and disarm their audience. How might teachers and students prepare (as best they can) for an event of this nature?

RESPONSIBILITY

1. A teacher must respond to an intrusion, especially with students caught off guard. How does a teacher "take matters in hand" and diffuse the attempted takeover?
2. How might each student protect himself or herself and others in this situation? Each student can influence the intruder—in positive and negative ways. What have you been told or taught about students' reactions and responses?

RESPONSE

1. How might a teacher remain calm, and help create a calm atmosphere in a situation as unnerving as a student entering a classroom to stage a potentially lethal plot? Also, Jay doesn't seem to exhibit good common sense; he's ready, seemingly, to simply act on his inclinations.
2. Do Terry and Marquis have an obligation to reveal the plot to a teacher or administrator? It needs no reminder, but students will not take the initiative in this situation and tattle on one another.

HOSTAGES IN A CLASSROOM

A disheveled male student enters a history class in progress at the local high school. He seems agitated, showing jerky movements, and his eyes dart around the room, trying to take in each student. He surveys the class again and again, and then looks back to the teacher, who has stopped the lesson. She notices that the student holds what looks like an explosive device with a pin. The intruder holds it at waist level because he wants everyone to see it. There is no way of telling if it might be a live explosive. The teacher remains calm.

"This is my class now," the intruder warns in a loud voice. "I'll tell you what to do for the rest of the day. Just don't try anything with me." A student with an explosive device might also shout out his purpose, making a statement such as "There's too many rich kids going to this school!" or "I think it's time we got rid of some of our bosses, especially Dean Williams and the big boss, Principal Willett!" Also, an intruder like this one may want a forum for his own ideas: He may say something like "Let's have a little talk about student rights in this school, and what we're going to do about it. It's now or never."

There may follow a tirade of perceived offenses that bother the intruder. This is a very serious step for the perpetrator, especially one with a live device. A student may have reached the end of his patience, as shown by this intruder when he says, "I'm not going to serve detentions or change schools or take the blame for someone else ever again. I'm not that stupid!"

Perceived insults, a threat to his well-being, or an event the intruder interprets as "the last straw"—or even "too many rich kids"—may be cited. Nothing bothers high school-age young adults like unfair rules or punishments, but most complain among like-minded fellow students. Few students take actions such as the one described.

Sometimes the more we think about a perceived insult or what we might regard as an unfair school rule or procedure or penalty, the more upset we may become. Rather than talking to an adult, a student who feels "pushed into a corner" once too often may respond illogically and inappropriately.

What steps are necessary to prepare a classroom of students for an upsetting, unexpected event with a potential for violence? What do experts advise in handling such situations?

Of major importance is how administrators may be contacted without the intruder's awareness. Also, an instructor might think about whether students in the classroom might appear to get out what seems to be homework and pretend to read or answer study questions on paper, for example.

READINESS

1. Students must avoid speaking to others, as well as to the hostage-taker. They should also avoid maintaining eye contact

with the stranger, unless it is evident that he or she wants an audience, and needs to be in the spotlight. Pick up clues from the hostage-taker in terms of what he or she wants.

2 There is no such thing as a hero in a situation of this nature. Rather, witnesses should remain as calm as they can and wait for an opportunity to allow the intruder to talk about his or her problem. Of course, everyone in the room must avoid trying to force the hostage-taker's hand or challenging the hostage-taker. Although the perpetrator exhibits strong emotions, the audience members must maintain control of their emotions and avoid verbalizing their reactions and opinions.

RESPONSIBILITY

1. What is a teacher's primary responsibility in this situation? What responsibilities might govern students' behaviors and their speaking out?
2. Have you witnessed or read about a situation as described in the second example? How did individual members of a group control themselves or others in reacting to the situation?

RESPONSE

1. (Teacher and students) Create and maintain a calm climate. Review some specific suggestions for doing this in advance of emergencies.

   (Teacher may address the intruder.) "Can you tell me what is wrong and how I can help? I can convey your request to office personnel or call the office and show you where it is." What response(s) may follow after the teacher's suggestions?
2. How does a teacher gauge what his or her response might be to a hostile intruder? If a person is disturbed, angry, and trying to maintain control of the situation he or she has created, what does an adult do? Pretend to accommodate all demands?

Note: an adult in this situation has to have an answer that may satisfy a disturbed person in a crisis situation that the person seeks to control. What advice might a trained professional offer?

3. Have you read about or witnessed staged events or heard any advice regarding hostage situations and angry perpetrators? Sharing these ideas may be helpful and lead to other suggestions from class members.

10

ELEMENTS OF EFFECTIVE LESSONS

There is concern among a group of parents about their children who attend Seaside Heights High School. The course guide notes "substantive mathematics content requiring high-level learning skills" in the advanced algebra classes. The parents question an advanced algebra in-class math objective related to a project, specifically an assignment to create posters illustrating graphing concepts and probability. They also discover upon questioning their young adults that one advanced algebra class set up and ran a café, serving coffee and snacks during student lunch periods to apply their knowledge of patterns and functions.

According to the instructor, Horace Warner, who is also the math department chair, the poster and café activities were examples of *experiential learning*. The café, in addition, provided an exercise to foster students' understanding and appreciation of studying advanced math concepts and functions that would challenge these particular students for the rest of the semester, if not the year's course of study.

One parent, Mrs. Martwick, questions her daughter Shelley and is surprised to learn the third-year student can complete "a lot" of her advanced algebra homework at school. After calling a number of homes in the Heights area, Martwick and a group of parents attend Seaside Heights' next school-board meeting. They raise concerns about whether specific skills are the focus in the high school math classes and if those skills are practiced and reviewed regularly. The adults also stress that their children need challenging classes with depth—in readiness for college placement tests and advanced education.

Board members understand their concerns, yet cannot respond to content questions about the district schools' departments. As a result, board members want to bring in a math specialist from the nearby state university to study and assess the Seaside Heights grades 9–12 math curriculum. The specialist will meet with the math department chair and also review students' standardized test scores. Warner will address specific concerns using his course objectives, as well as his priorities in math classroom work. Martwick and the other parents are relieved that there will be follow-up to address their concerns.

When the researcher questions students in the advanced algebra courses, he learns that students feel "challenged" by Warner's homework assignments. Apparently, Warner reviews reasoning skills as they solve each homework problem. Students feel the textbook is difficult and the problems assigned are usually complex, though thought provoking and satisfying when completed. The young adults know they cannot expect school to be "fun" and understand that their readiness for college is important. Moreover, most students expressed surprise at the poster assignment and the café during the Friday lunch periods. In fact, a good number of Warner's students worried about whether the coming week's advanced algebra class would include a review of the assigned problems, since they missed the class in working on the projects.

Warner suspected that students' reactions to the out-of-class assignments might raise questions, and he felt those activities provided learning opportunities. He knew students would return to math classes more committed to the rigorous units ahead. That was his plan: to allow students the experience of applying their skills, knowledge, and concepts from previous math classes to advanced algebra, and to help them understand that more enjoyable assignments may not challenge their math knowledge and set the stage for upcoming units in advanced algebra. The instructor explains that he follows the curriculum guidelines: he chaired the committee that created the objectives for the school's math offerings. He stands by the legitimacy and standards, as well as the rigor, built into most courses taught in his department.

The diligent math instructor states that his lesson plans for students always include a clear purpose for each class, each day; an activity for which students assume responsibility (small-group discussion of solutions and/or a review of homework problems); and anticipation of new material and application of previous learning units.

READINESS

1. Is a review of previous math concepts and material, plus reference to previous units of study, necessary in order for students to move into new learning units?
2. How might each unit of math study offer an opportunity for students to "reach beyond the textbook"?
3. Some teachers use a daily course goal, which is written on the board and referred to throughout the class. How does this help students learn?
4. Should all instructors distribute a review sheet or an outline of material for students for each class meeting?

RESPONSIBILITY

1. Explain the role of school leaders in terms of clear, specific learning objectives for each course taught in school.

2. How might school leaders encourage teachers to evolve daily lessons that engage students and appeal to their interests, as well as helping them acquire skills?
3. What methods may help students learn, along with providing a change of pace in their classes? For example, some teachers use guest speakers; films that apply to a unit; or materials from a variety of sources, including supplemental textbooks, newspapers and magazines, and excerpts from national test samples.
4. If outlines and worksheets follow a teacher's plan for the day's lesson, is this making the units of study too easy? Might students create study guide questions related to some units and question one another in teams, for example?
5. How important are monthly assignment sheets in instructors' course planning? Does every teacher need to create and distribute these?
6. What methods of reviewing material for testing may also prompt students' interest and enjoyment?

RESPONSE

1. How often might teachers suggest a change in textbooks or learning objectives in view of new material that may be more timely or connected to new computer applications?
2. Provide examples of students' progress in a course, whether participation in answering questions or asking them, attaining higher grades than in previous units, or involvement in the lessons via group work. Connect these to changes in a teacher's approach or students' embracing additional responsibility for their own learning. What other factors promote students' involvement in classes?
3. If you have taught or visited classes in which students offered insights about the textbook, in-class outlines and worksheets, specific class activities, homework, projects, and tests, what feedback do you recall?

4. Most students enjoy active involvement in class—dramatizing a short-story character's plight, planning dialogue between characters in a book analysis, or relating books read to their own experience. These activities may not teach skills to students—or do they? What percentage of time spent in math, science, English, history/geography, and other subjects might be devoted to student involvement? How does a teacher gauge the benefit of these activities, as opposed to the learning of skills?

5. Is it necessary for teachers to evolve a specific objective for each class meeting? How might students benefit from an instructor's specifying what the daily objective is? Objectives, for example, might start with these sample phrases: *to show, to compile a list of, to review, to explain, to outline,* and *to practice the skills of.*

11

FEMALE STUDENTS FIGHTING

A female student may initiate a fight with another female student, especially in grades 10 through 12, due to perceived differences between them. If a student excels in a specialty area such as modeling or dance and students do not know her, they may assume she lives a more privileged life than most other students. A female student may respond inappropriately to the exceptional student or to friends, hoping to elicit evidence of others' perceptions which match her own.

Also, a girl who looks and acts more mature or who is advanced in school coursework or is the recipient of academic honors may remain isolated from others or draw some negative female attention. The fact that a gifted student seems older, or more poised or privileged than fellow students, can also be a source of other girls' criticism.

Francine Lancaster, for example, exhibits unusual abilities in dance and joins the city dance company in *The Nutcracker* each year. Her joining the cast came about simply because she took lessons from the best dancers. Articles about the production have appeared in local and national newspapers, and a magazine has written about

Lancaster's unusual gift in ballet. A student who does not know her may misinterpret her silence in the classes they share, assuming Francine to be snobbish and aloof.

"You think you're so hot, don't you?" asks Gloria Taylor, addressing Francine after class as they stand at their adjacent lockers, dialing combinations.

"No, I don't understand this textbook and the explanations in class—or the application questions," admits Francine.

"But you're Miss Perfect."

"No, I'm not," insists the dancer. "I thought government would be an interesting class elective; I haven't a lot of extra time to put into the class."

"You're not serious! I know you're a good student."

"Yes, I am serious. My grades in this class are all C-minuses!" In this brief conversation, Francine's honesty has disarmed Gloria's assumptions.

Girls may also gather a group of female friends to confront a student whom they feel is a potential threat to a boy-girl relationship with a member of the group.

Valerie Williams has dated Terrell Manning several times in the past month—when he is not practicing basketball or scouting teams in the North Suburban League.

Valerie is certain she and Terrell are tight, a couple. One lunch period, however, she notices Terrell is not eating with two of his teammates who usually join him to talk about sports. Instead, Valerie notices Joylynn De Spain sitting next to Terrell; the two are alone at a table, and her anger surfaces. "I'll get her," she whispers aloud. That girl is in for a surprise!"

Valerie plans to "take care" of the situation as quickly as possible. She must put Joylynn "in her place" as well as warn her and scare her, if possible. What better way is there than to gather five or six friends—Joyce Davis, Hernetta Mabley, Gwennie Merritt, and Cornelia Johnson. These friends will help her; she's sure of it. They will each make it clear: Terrell Manning belongs to Valerie.

Another problem surfaces at times among girls, especially upper-division students and lower-division students in the same class. In some situations, the students' maturity levels differ; the experiences of the two groups in many cases differ, and the girls' physical skills may be different.

Period 7, Section G300 is an afternoon gym class at Williamsburg High School. School scheduling has grouped together in this class all girls from grades 9 through 12 who have unusual schedules that leave them no other available time for the required class. These unusual schedules might include one with no available free periods; one that includes an excused "leave early" permit for job experience; or one belonging to an underclassman taking upper-division courses.

The class invariably separates into freshmen/sophomores and the upperclass students, with the upper-division girls excelling or winning at each sports unit. The underclassmen are less familiar with the sports and they flounder, much to the amusement of the older girls. It leads to a lot of less-than-good-natured joking and mimicking.

Miss Chandler, the PE instructor, has created mixed teams of the two groups, but the upper-division students separate and exchange places, telling the underclassmen that's the way they want it. These situations increase chances for fights, disagreements, and hard feelings that may escalate easily into physical confrontations.

Chandler receives a number of calls from parents about the class's unusual nature due to the two groups of students. The older students make fun of the awkward and sometimes unskilled younger students, who have not had the PE classes the older students have had. But Chandler does not want to make too much fuss about the differences, because these girls can't transfer out. What are her choices?

The gym instructor might proceed with a "straight talk" approach, mandating that each student in the class show respect for and encourage the underclass students' efforts—or fail the class (for lack of sportsmanlike conduct). She can assign detentions or schedule a talk between Dean Lucas and the class about any verbal sarcasm or critical comments that have been shouted for everyone else in the class to hear. Or Chandler might try to pinpoint a ringleader who starts or encourages the verbal criticisms. She would also prefer it if the groups worked out the issues themselves, using class time—but she knows it is unlikely that the upperclassmen will take the initiative, even if she suggests it; and it is equally unlikely that the underclassmen will challenge the upperclassmen. What advice might outsiders offer to Chandler?

When students perceive other students as "different" in terms of their abilities or skills, their interests, or their life experiences, problems may result. When students become jealous of their friends talking to or spending time with students they regard as either special or close friends—or their dating partners—problems usually result. The conflicts pitting older students against younger students are unfair-advantage situations; the underclassmen are not ready to compete with an experienced and older group of students.

Can we apprise students of alternative behaviors when they believe they must act out, perhaps inappropriately, in response to strong feelings or a perceived need to assert themselves—or because advantages of age and experience will "win" every time?

12

INTRUDERS IN THE SCHOOL BUILDING

SHONDA SANDERS' PLAN

Shonda Sanders has known Derrick Williams only a few weeks, but feels her love for him is "so strong it will last forever." Both are high school seniors, though Shonda attends East Bridgeton High School and Derrick is a student at Salisbury-Andover High School in the next county, north of East Bridgeton.

Sanders' friend Cornelia Walsh also attends Salisbury and, coincidentally, eats during the first lunch period, as does Derrick. Cornelia feels obligated to tell her friend that she has seen Derrick eating lunch with Gloria Cooper this week. The couple also sat in the adjoining outdoor courtyard area of the cafeteria, where it is less noisy, though one can be seen by everyone in the cafeteria. Cornelia decides to omit the detail that the two sat close to one another; she had noted, with alarm, how cozy they seemed.

Shonda doesn't take her friend's news well and immediately plans to confront Gloria, to "put her in her place." She will make it clear she does not want the two eating lunch together or socializing and will remind Gloria, "Someone is watching you," at her school.

Her plan is to leave school immediately, drive to Salisbury-Andover, and talk to her rival.

Should a teacher or someone else stop her, she plans to say, "I'm going to a dental appointment but I've lost my permit pass. I'm sorry, but I am late, and it hurts. Call my mother." She realizes if she leaves through the PE doors that open onto the parking lots in back of the school, no one will notice. But there is also a possibility that someone at Salisbury will ask for her ID. It takes several minutes before Shonda creates an explanation: "My mom and I are moving here soon. She's divorced. She wants me to finish high school at Salisbury and then go to Andover Valley (a community college)—but Mom works and couldn't be here today. I am so excited I just had to see SA. I might even know someone here!"

Shonda realizes how smart a talker she is when explaining her ideas nonstop and overwhelming others. She thinks of herself as very creative when she uses details about people she knows to make a story convincing. She may even create a story about why they are moving, when they will relocate, what she will miss, and how much she needs to just see the school and "look around" before they move.

"I'll make up stuff as I drive," she says aloud.

Note: Shonda's thought processes and actions, and her plan to make up stories to suit her purpose, are not unusual for young adults; whatever consequences follow her actions may well surprise Shonda.

ROB MILLER'S PREDICAMENT

A male student opens the front door of Riverside High School, and enters a small reception area where an adult male sits at a desk. He stands immediately to greet and question the visitor, asking to see an entrance pass or ID, which is required of visitors by all district schools.

"My girlfriend is in class now, but we've got to talk," explains Rob Miller. "That's why I'm here."

"We don't allow anyone without a pass in this building," explains Llewellyn Meyer, a social studies instructor.

"This is *important*," Rob insists, with impatience. "It will take only a minute."

"We've got our rules, just like all schools," repeats Meyer sternly. "This is a security checkpoint. You are on school district property. One phone call and you are reported *trespassing*, young man."

"When *can* I see her?" asks Rob, who is impatient and angry, though willing to wait for the next bell.

"At 3:30, the end of our school day," Meyer states simply.

"This is stupid, plain stupid," insists Rob. "I've never heard of anything like this."

"School policy," reminds Meyer.

"I can see why people break into schools," the visitor mumbles.

"That comment goes on record right now, young man," warns Meyer. "And I need to see your ID!" When Rob hesitates, Meyer is quick to remind him: "An ID—now!"

JAIME DELGADO'S DILEMMA

Jaime Delgado enters the Hazelton Middle School building about thirty minutes earlier than the buses one morning. Luck is with him: there is no one in the back entrance, which is open for the buses.

Normally there are several coaches waiting for buses to drop off students; they talk and drink coffee, as all coaches' offices encircle the wing of this corridor.

Jaime wants to talk with Mr. Belding, the PE coach who, he feels, has soured the high school coach on Jaime. This is the second year he has not been chosen to play basketball at Carver High, and he cannot overlook what he perceives was a slight. More than anything, Jaime wants to play basketball on the Carver team, which always makes the play-offs for the state championship. But if he confronts the coach verbally, he knows he may end up dealing with Dean

Wentz if he gets into "an argument or something." Then, suddenly, he gets what he calls "a one-million-dollar idea."

He smiles, thinking about entering the athletic-office complex and "kind of messing up Belding's office." Jaime feels this is a "real genius move" because there will be no one to suspect him. He has already fulfilled his mission by entering the building unnoticed; and, if he hurries, he can trash the office and get away before the kids get off the buses and everybody enters the building. This way, no one knows anything. No one can identify him. "I'll zip out of here in no time at all," he whispers aloud. "It's so perfect. You are a genius, Del," he reminds himself.

KYLE LAWSON'S DECISION

Kyle Lawson, a loner, never liked school and seemed not to enjoy the company of others. He ate lunch alone and then used the computer room or a "continuous chess" local TV channel in the junior-senior lounge to pass his time. He didn't seem to fit into any student groups.

At age twenty-two, he is now a man with a purpose, ready to "make a statement" at Washington High School. He will go back and let "all of them" remember who he is and that he dared to interfere with their "perfect" school.

Lawson's current job history is one of "not communicating with supervisors or peers" in four different job settings. With customers in a department store, his attitude was supercilious. He has been asked to leave all four jobs. Lawson blames Washington High School.

He enters the back of the school building, intent on getting "them" to remember him, a graduate. He still knows how to enter the loading-dock area of the large school and walk through the huge building to the main hallway. Lawson carries a weapon; there are no detectors on his route.

Students file out of classes as the tone sounds to change classes, and the hallways are noisy with conversations. It makes him slightly nervous, anxious, to be in the midst of school again.

Sara Pritchard, a student, notices Lawson's sport jacket and chinos, then his facial expression. The visitor looks determined to get to a destination—but also like he is "in another world," as she sees him. She asks herself "Who is he? Have I seen him before? I don't think so; I'd remember."

Guy Terrell and Jason McNulty, friends, are talking about trig homework as both notice the stranger. "Who is that dude?" McNulty asks. "A slob, I believe," Jason answers. "And no books, either. What's his problem?" They exchange a brief laugh from across the hall and walk on.

Reid Donellan and his girlfriend Shelly Peterson also notice the stranger. "He gives me the chills. Look at him—why didn't someone write him up? His jacket is filthy, too," remarks Shelly. Reid is a class leader and approaches Lawson, asking, "Can I help you get somewhere?" And the answer comes immediately: "Not now, buddy." As quickly as he answers, Lawson withdraws a gun and aims it at his own head, the gun touching his temple. Only seconds slip by as he pulls the trigger, taut, at his head.

READINESS

1. This item refers to the suicide in the example above.

   A crisis counselor or counselors will be available to speak to individuals and/or small or large groups of students as a result of Lawson's death. How else might school staff members and administrators address the suicide? What interventions may help students understand this event to the best of their ability and respond to their shock, as well as promoting their recovery?

2. Parents and students need information via a bulletin and/or the invitation to an open forum with administrators, to review occasions when a stranger or several strangers enter a school building. Have sporting events been the scene of any emergency or crisis situations in your experience? Has a stranger suddenly appeared in a school you know of? How was the

stranger dealt with? When recalling Lawson's presence in a school building, parents might be reminded to help school leaders by explaining to their children that they insist the children immediately report to an adult or adults their seeing a stranger, specifying where the person or persons was/were seen.

3. A motivational speaker might address all students at the beginning of each school year to remind them about behavior; grades; good judgment; safety issues; and controlling their tendency to make impulsive decisions; that is, to react immediately rather than thinking through a situation—a tendency illustrated by Shonda. An outside speaker's use of straight talk and some humor, plus examples to explain important points, might be more acceptable to students than the same ideas delivered by school personnel. Also, a well-respected coach of any sport can usually motivate students toward appropriate behavior, as well as inspiring listeners.

4. A copy of school rules and procedures should be sent home to all district parents/guardians as each new year begins, along with contact names and phone numbers. Their input about "safe school" standards and practices should be requested.

5. Classroom teachers might engage students in panel or group discussions of "safe school" rules and appropriate behaviors at the beginning of a term or year, if appropriate to their age level.

6. As the school year begins, class leaders and/or members of sports teams might remind and encourage students to comply with school rules in a special assembly. Also, members of the school newspaper staff could use every newspaper issue to focus on one or two "safe school" rules simply by listing them, and boxing these reminders as an ad.

7. The bottom line is the hiring of a trained, full-time, armed school safety officer.

8. Committed staff members willing to serve on hall duty, who will face challenges as Meyer does, should be utilized. Though he seems harsh with Rob, would any adult complain about his manner?

9. Administrators might invite a group of students interested in theater arts and/or speech activities to portray a scenario about a stranger at school, illustrating appropriate student responses and/or behavior during a class assembly, for example.

10. The importance of reporting rumors of potential school disruption, or any event out of the ordinary that might harm school personnel or students (a fight, destructive activity, plans to disrupt classes or athletic events, etc.), should be emphasized.

11. Review any school crisis incidents or events in your experience that were handled with adequate coverage and containment due to meticulous preparation in advance. Or review an event that was unanticipated and/or destructive or upsetting, stating how the event might have been handled.

RESPONSIBILITY

1. Do your school district's handbook for students and manual for faculty and staff include a safe-strategies check-off list in case of emergencies (e.g., "Close, lock windows")? Are these reminders posted in all classrooms?

2. Who has reported to parents and area residents a description of an emergency event and how or why it occurred at a school with which you are familiar? Why is this report necessary? Was it effective?

3. Do faculty and staff members summon a district safety officer, if available, to assume command of a crisis situation or event if it occurs? Provide details of a situation you are aware of in a school setting, plus specifics about who handled it and how well the event or situation was controlled.

4. Did members of a safety or crisis-response team meet at a prearranged location to review and contain an event or situation, occurring on school property, with which you are familiar? Who decides which measures are necessary in a specific

situation or event? What is the response mode expected of students and adults?

5. Describe a recent practice devoted to an emergency drill or a school-wide exit of the building(s), and how successful the practice was. Note: Refer to noise level, slow or expeditious exiting of the building(s), whether people remained or failed to remain with their assigned classes or groups, and so on. How might you improve the drill, when the next one occurs? Students need to know how seriously building leaders view safety issues.

6. If you were a member of a faculty-staff committee planning an assembly for students to review effective and appropriate safe behaviors during an emergency, what behaviors would you mention and explain?

RESPONSE

1. Do authorized visitors display a badge or wear a lanyard provided by the school's main office in a school with which you are familiar?

2. How might adults encourage students to avoid approaching a stranger in the school or on school property until they know the stranger is welcome and safe to talk with?

3. What school safety measures might be implemented if a stranger like Jaime gained access to the school building or buildings with which you are familiar? What features make a building safe? Identify safety personnel or systems utilized by the school or schools you know of. Relying on the fact that someone in the building will notice a stranger and respond appropriately is not a foolproof strategy.

4. Are classrooms locked when not in use in the buildings with which you are familiar? Why or why not?

5. What safety measures might encompass the school parking lots (recalling Shonda's expectation of access)? What parking lot features compromise school safety, in your experience or view?

6. Reviewing your own experience with strangers on-site (an assessment team, for example, or members of the local school board or workers assessing an area or repairing a window, flooring or ceiling), how and when might school personnel engage students to follow appropriate, safe behavior?

13

POTENTIAL SCHOOL DROPOUTS

Finish School or Full-Time Job?

Bettina Wilson elected to obtain an early school-release permit this semester to work part-time at a local big-box store. She started two months ago, and, as with all new employees, received at each month's end an overall final job-performance rating. Her rating read *Excellent* for both months.

Recently, she learned that a full-time position in the children's department would soon open. Bettina immediately wondered if she should quit school now and apply for the full-time position. She has worked in that department and considered the experience enjoyable.

Would her paycheck reflect *double* the amount she now earns if she sought and received full-time status? School is boring in her view, as she tells her parents. They object, insisting she stay in school until she graduates; they point out that she might remain in low-paying positions the rest of her life.

"Earning a diploma is only the beginning of your career," insists Derrick Wilson. "You may find additional training for whatever you want to specialize in offered at Lawrence Community College, or even on another campus. But you need the diploma in order to enroll, even at Lawrence." This is not what Bettina wanted to hear.

Her father adds, "I always thought you had the potential to do anything you wanted; your abilities are much better than mine. Don't cut yourself off, Betty: I guarantee you will regret it later on. Look at Howie Chance—he quit high school and regrets it to this day. He wanted to specialize in welding; well, the community colleges offer a full program in the one area he thinks he would have excelled in."

Mrs. Wilson decides she will call the school and speak with her daughter's counselor; surely she can recommend that Bettina contact someone who will provide another negative view of quitting before graduation.

Students sometimes regard a full-time job as their freedom from school, and relish the fact that they no longer take orders from teachers, counselors, and other adults. A problem that may quickly surface, however, is in the form of the supervisors and managers who are part of any work setting. These individuals may disappoint Bettina as much as school adults.

Friends may encourage students they know to quit, without realizing that they themselves are unaware of others' potential in specific areas of interest. They do no one a favor advocating leaving school. Earning a diploma is the start of something important to Bettina, which she doesn't see now—a better job in an area she wants to stay with may be in her future, but only if she stays in school and graduates.

Is college *necessary* when career success beckons?

Kyle Miller and Renee Dowling experience a new event in their lives; they started dating almost a year ago and are now committed to one another. Both feel theirs is a true, *forever* relationship, and each wonders about marriage. Are they ready for a lifetime commitment?

Kyle had planned on college, before he met Renee. He is a high-school junior who might well succeed in higher education because he has the ability to continue his good academic work. He has maintained a B-plus grade average with the precollege major, looking toward the state university at Charleston. He thought about playing soccer there, having been named to the Division 1 team by the city newspaper.

Renee envisioned a future in which she would marry "someday," but she didn't expect to meet and get to know Kyle. Now she cannot imagine being without him. Renee has no immediate educational or job goals, other than her familiarity with health care and health services, her mother's field of expertise.

But she also wonders at times about how she might succeed as a dental hygienist; Asbury Community College offers a premedical career program with skills training, a jump-start preparation for the full medical program at the local university that will follow. Renee knows there will be a lot of work ahead if she wants to pursue that goal. However, she can imagine herself with a dentist who wants to utilize his or her skills on restorations, crown and bridge work, and dentures, while she fulfills the hygienist's role.

Kyle still wants to discuss what is available for him by talking with the college representatives who seem to visit the high school athletic department almost every other week. He is certain he will retain his talents and skills in soccer, a sport he has excelled in for years. On the other hand, Renee is the most wonderful person he has ever met. Spending the rest of his life with Renee would be worth any sacrifice, as he envisions it. What is his decision? Might he lose Renee if he waits until finishing college?

Can Kyle have all that he wants now, at this time of his life, he wonders? Should he talk to the representatives, or quit athletics and try the world of work? As he sees it, he could easily set up a soccer-training school for kids. With his reputation, he would draw a lot of interest locally—but it's a *now* thing, as he knows. He's never experienced these complexities: the girl of his dreams and a career that would be successful if he started right now, while his ranking is high in the state.

On the other hand, he thought about college because his dad specialized in business administration. He wants his son to pursue a college *career*. Should he continue his education? Is everything that he wants possible for him to achieve? He has the name recognition right now. Kyle is not one to wait too long to make a decision, but this time he is stumped.

READINESS

1. Statistics prove the value of education in terms of personal job satisfaction, advancement in the field of one's interest, and compensation. Locate the data, if possible, and use it to tell students the disadvantages of dropping out. Better yet, post or duplicate information revealing the value of education over a lifetime of work. Retirees have valuable perspectives to offer about education in terms of their work experiences and satisfaction; they can offer specifics about their jobs and, perhaps, the need to increase one's skills and knowledge before and after securing a position.

2. Use reliable information from government agencies and other sources to provide a view against dropping out of school before graduation. Note: One out of three high school students drop out each school year.

3. List ten reasons why education is the best predictor of lifetime success, happiness, and personal well-being. Facts and statistics may reveal the realities students have not considered. Review any relevant data with students.

4. Use facts and figures to specify programs of study during and after military service.

5. Be alert, so that you can pinpoint skills in which specific students may need additional one-on-one instruction, or supplemental, specialized courses; seek dialogue with a student's counselor about remediation or additional courses of study. Point out for students the reality of the *testing* that is required in some professional areas: physicians must take exams on their medical knowledge every ten years. Accountants also face regular retesting related to their field as long as they want to remain licensed and working.

6. Investigate available work-study programs, and talk with students about them.

RESPONSIBILITY

1. If you hear a student criticize a subject or teacher or a student who dislikes school and disagrees with "all the rules" and responsibilities, call home and mention the facts to parents. The issues and perceptions may need discussing with a counselor, a favorite teacher, or parents. A student may need to consider another point of view—before deciding to quit school.

2. If a student complains about course work and reveals test scores and grades that are lower than is desirable, contact a student's counselor to check the available standardized test scores. Students who criticize or complain may need remediation in a specific subject area. Pursue remediation with the student, as needed, and suggest ongoing dialogue between student and counselor to encourage progress at grade level in every subject area, if possible.

3. All adults who interact with students might be reminded to remain alert to their complaints about school—in order to provide necessary discussion of their perspectives and, perhaps, opinions that students might respect.

4. Parents and relatives are in a good position to influence students' opinions and choices, encouraging their efforts. Adults' perspectives are valuable, and young people need reminders about their skills, abilities, and interests related to specific subjects. An article might be written for the local newspaper which offers adults ideas about students' ongoing need for dialogue with adults throughout their school careers.

5. A school leader might write a column or article for the local newspaper or the bulletin from the district office about the importance of education, in which students could also be encouraged to take advantage of special services and testing

opportunities in the district. There might be additional opportunities for students to receive encouragement and remediation, as needed, as well as the benefits of an adult's perspective and knowledge.

RESPONSE

1. Review the lives and career choices of individuals you know or know of (but whose names you do not reveal). Tell their stories; explain their choices. Include opposites: those who attended college and earned a degree, and those who did not but who were still successful in their chosen fields. Allow students to see the value of both. Most "self-made" individuals without education worked hard at a specialty, whether a pastime or a chosen vocation, and proved successful.

2. Engage in a one-on-one discussion with a student. This will allow you to know his or her specific situation: Is the student failing a course? Does she dislike her teacher or the subject, or does he dislike the students he sits nearest? There may exist factors that create a problem with a class or instructor, or with other students.

3. Set up a career/job fair; locate the work-study program details, if available.

4. Recruit community people to talk to students about the value of education. This could include businesspeople and employers, and business owners who did not pursue post-high school study.

14

STUDENTS WHO DISLIKE SCHOOL

"How's school?" is a familiar question that parents ask their children. However, what response might another adult whom students do not know receive to the question? The following are a few answers I've heard: "It's so boring. Class, homework, test—that's it. You *have* to be here. It's boring. Period." Another student replied, "I'm not in a good group," and kept on walking down the hall. One young adult with a heavy load of books said simply, "No one likes school. I don't like school."

Questioning teachers about isolating one student in particular who has caught their attention and concern brought several professionals' perspectives. One instructor mentioned Marco, who needed to be the center of attention during classes; he used jokes and shouted out whatever comments occurred to him. Thus far, a behavioral referral to his class counselor (copy to the dean) had not yet been acted upon. Another teacher mentioned a student who looked like an adult male, though still a high school sophomore. His wearing apparel might have reflected cultural expectations which set him apart from most other boys in school. He wore dark leather shoes and cloth trousers, instead of the ubiquitous worn jeans with patches or holes and billowing cloth shirts. The instructor felt he was ready for what might be a formal work setting after school. Thus far in the semester, the student had turned in no assignments.

Female students were also mentioned, including Lauren, whose inattention in class was overt. She chatted and whispered, gesticulated and eye-rolled, passed notes when warned about talking, and did not seem to pay attention. Occasionally she might allow others to hear a comment to her friend in a nearby row; the instructor heard her say "This is stupid!" Her giggling and laughing drew warnings from the teacher, who would call her home when she had time to do so. Rovena, a junior, seemed serious about the class (U.S. history), though troubled or angry or unsure about what to write down. She seemed to pay attention but was easily distracted, impatient, or frustrated. Might her difficulty be a learning disability or problems with reading, since the class used the textbook extensively? It was early in the school year and the instructor, who was concerned, would soon talk to the girl and also call her home. The teacher utilized worksheet outlines for students to fill in during class, a convenient method for test review.

Students who dislike school isolate such specifics as "This school is too big"; others say a school has too many cliques, that there are "authority types" in the main office or too many rules, or even that there are "too many rich kids" attending. Although students may not specify class size, classes of twenty-five or more students may not be best for all subjects and also make individualizing instruction difficult. Other students have less than adequate preparation for high school requirements, let alone college work: Who wants to attend classes if the material is unfamiliar or one has no background for it?

In addition, no single learning method or style of teaching is ideal for the majority of students; some are visual learners, while others do well with books. Still others shine when there are hands-on problems, projects, or experiments for which individual students are responsible. Computer instruction may not necessarily replace teachers who can lead students through an in-hand outline or review the steps of a word problem in math. Yet computers can teach students some of the skills they need; however, what are those skills?

One student sees no difference between *decimal* and *decisive* or between *consternation* and *concentration*. Students with learning problems may respond well when a problem is detected, with the one-on-one help of a specialist.

I recall a high school graduate with a good job in the health-care industry, assigned to describing the specific benefits that individual clients with health issues were entitled to. He loved his job. In spite of the paperwork he provided the state, there was no remediation for his weaknesses: poor vocabulary skills, weakness in spelling, and the inability to write a paragraph. His paragraphs might extend for several pages, with no breaks, no focus, and no purpose sentence. One other example might illustrate one of his problems: he thought *idea* and *ideal* were the same word, and used *ideal* most often because it had the extra letter at the end.

Students who dislike school: how many do you know, and how do they adapt to daily instruction? What are your perceptions regarding these students? Consider personality and behavioral traits; classroom attentiveness or disruption; verbalizations in or outside of classes; number of absences; and parents' impressions. How might you define *a student who dislikes school*?

Think of student behaviors, attitudes, and verbalizations that reveal their dislike. What professionals inside or outside school might change students' perceptions in order to enrich their academic experiences? How prevalent are negative attitudes toward school and/or specific classes, in your experience? What steps or changes might diminish extremely negative student perceptions and feelings? Course changes? A requirement waiver? A change of teacher or class? In your experience, what course of action has an administrator or other specialist suggested for specific students? How do we enlist parents' help and support so every student at every grade level achieves at his or her best possible level?

RESPONSE

1. Teachers or any adults in a school community who encounter the pattern or frequency of a student's or students' negativity about school, a class or classes, teachers, a student or group of students, requirements, or bus drivers or other adult personnel can influence a student in a positive manner and encourage more appropriate responses. Note: A district newsletter might well include an article themed "Attitude Is Everything," utilizing quotes from coaches, sports heroes, business people, and so on.
2. You may not change student attitudes, but providing an "open forum" for discussion when possible, or addressing complaints and any misperceptions or miscommunications, may help. Show your interest and enthusiasm for the subject.
3. Consider a shift in instructional approaches; you might arrange for student groups to present key ideas in a chapter or review new material, which may point the direction toward the next lesson.
4. Evolve a behavioral contract, informing parents, as necessary; outline desired changes and continue to "catch" students doing well, changing behavior, and so on. Report weekly to parents; create specific goals for students to achieve.
5. Show the value of the subject you teach (skills acquired, awareness heightened, etc.).
6. Notice and respond to positive behavior or changes in a student's attitudes; academic achievement and progress make a learner feel proud of his or her own efforts, even if the learner doesn't share these perceptions—it's hard to beat that good feeling of a *job* well done.
7. Keep in mind the key words: *acknowledge, encourage,* and *support* student efforts.
8. Consider allowing the last five minutes of class as a time to wrap up with a review, to keep students on target for the next class meeting.

READINESS

1. Observe students and listen to them (as well as teaching the curriculum).
2. Discuss effective strategies to combat negativity during an early department or faculty meeting.
3. Create an open class discussion with students on the theme of "Let's Make It a Positive Year"; compile students' perceptions and ideas, as needed, for discussion with other faculty and staff.
4. Become acquainted with individual students' interests, especially sports and national sports heroes, who sometimes provide opinions that may help students.
5. If possible, relate the subject taught and skills required to any jobs and careers with which you are familiar.
6. Consider whether a local businessperson might be willing to review with students the necessity of education as he or she has experienced it in a chosen career.

RESPONSIBILITY

1. Ready students for graduation, post-high school training and higher education, and jobs and careers.
2. Alert students to the positive results of their education (knowledge; readiness for additional study and/or training; specific jobs or careers).
3. Raise concerns with parents, who may review positive attitudes and growth toward maturity. ("You don't have to like requirements, but you can learn to put maximum efforts into anything you do.") Allow parents to connect academics to continuing education, jobs, and careers.
4. Review any negative patterns you notice in students' speech and tone, body language, facial expressions, and so on.
5. Raise issues that impact an individual student's perceptions about the class, the material, policies and practices,

"personality conflicts," and so forth in a private meeting; draw in parents, if necessary (and if possible).

5. Meet and discuss class behaviors, attitudes, and so on with the school psychologist, the counselor, or other personnel, as indicated.

6. Always point out the student's strengths, abilities, skills, and talents.

7. Apply educational efforts to any jobs and career areas that a student may show interest in.

8. Consider showing your interest and enthusiasm about the subject you teach to students.

9. Take "knowledge breaks" periodically to offer insights about the subject or talk about well-known theorists and their contributions to the field of study; that is, "Did you know . . . ?"

10. Review a previous lesson, perhaps tying it in to the current day's work. This creates continuity.

11. Make time to review and reteach material. If students succeed in academic areas, their achievement can change their attitudes. Review and reteaching may bring success to students who most need the two.

PARENTS' ROLES

Parents may be the best adults to review a student's attitude and performance in a class. They may set goals and rewards for their children as no one else can; parents can also explain their appreciation of learning and succeeding during their own lives. Most of us regard successful jobs as one of the payoffs of our education; students may need a review of jobs and careers that lie ahead and their relationship to learning that happens now. Maybe a student with a less-than-satisfactory attitude needs reminders about "the big picture" and his or her role in a job or career. Enlist the help of parents and keep them apprised of a student's progress or shortfalls.

SCHOOL LEADER FOCUS

1. What factors are you familiar with that most affect a student's negative attitude toward school and/or classes? Might these include specific personality traits, the number of absences, behavioral problems, problems at home—or others you can specify?

2. What examples of attitude changes (from negative to positive attitudes) toward academics and/or school have you witnessed? What caused the changes?

3. As an administrator, how might you help create the appropriate tone or atmosphere for an effective school? Please describe your goals for the school's tone and atmosphere.

4. What methods can be used to alter students' sometimes negative attitudes and perceptions? Can you offer an example or examples? Might small-group meetings and discussions help? Counselor advisement? Discussions with specific personnel outside the school setting?

5. Do you feel that enlisting the help of parents and/or a school counselor helps change student perceptions? Can you provide an example?

6. Describe the steps you, personally, have taken to change specific students' attitudes. Is it a case of "each student is completely unique"?

7. What potential benefit might guest speakers from the community bring, especially in speaking about their own job successes?

15

THE SCHOOL
SAFETY OFFICER

Consider the number of school crisis situations that have been publicized in news stories; these crises have been provoked by intruders who sought to disrupt the normal daily routine, students with grudges who carried weapons onto campus, and groups or gangs at odds with other groups. Many adults have questioned whether individual school buildings and their campuses are secure. If you think about it, you might conclude that we can and probably should delegate school safety issues to experts, such as a district or school safety officer who is a member of the local police force.

Why would there be a need for an outsider to monitor a school's safety plan and suggest improvements? School administrators' schedules are already full, and each day brings another set of problems, and people with whom they must meet. And teachers are engaged in planning and delivering daily instructional services. Their job is instruction of students rather than responding to crisis events.

A school security officer's areas of responsibility include the school buildings and campus, as well as the parking areas. Police personnel are the trained security experts. Consider what these experts might accomplish: analyzing problem areas unique to each school and suggesting remedies; planning and executing safety practice drills, to include students and staff in the buildings; systematically checking every inside door, as well as doors leading outside; developing a plan to engage all students in submitting safety suggestions, with rewards for those ideas implemented; creating and leading a school safety committee and engaging the members to recommend changes as needed; and posing "What if . . . ?" scenarios for building adults to review how to handle safety issues, which could also be a means of engaging students in the school's safety plans.

A school safety officer would create a school safety plan individualized to a specific school—every school potentially needs a plan suited to its buildings. The opportunity to meet with parent groups and explain new "safe school site" measures would be a chance to engage additional interested volunteers to share a role in maintaining safe buildings. A police officer is the ideal school safety expert who can become familiar with school staff members as well as students—and recognize a stranger on-site. Who can improve on the efforts of schools that have a police officer on duty, daily, on campus?

In addition, police who are school security officers attend conferences and conventions to maintain awareness about safe school problems and remedies. These personnel might also publish safety bulletins for in-school use. It is the school security officer who might write a school's safety plan, with specific goals and recommendations, as necessary. The security officer might also offer workshops periodically to review issues such as crisis events in the classroom. Distributing school building checklists tailored to the specific features of each school would extend the security officer's procedures to adults who might want to assist in school safety plans and methods.

School Safety Officer K. Horton is the deputy school resource officer for the fourteen Franklin County (North Carolina) schools. These include 701 pupils in 8 elementary schools, 3 middle schools, 3 high schools, and a creative education center.

When students are in school, so is Horton, wherever he is needed. A formidable figure, Horton softens considerably when talking about students. His rapport with young people was illustrated at a Saturday morning school-safety expo event: several students spent time greeting him and talking with him, though the event drew mostly adults.

Bulky in a uniform over safety apparel, the school resource officer appears loaded down with what appears to be a heavy gun, plus a night stick and a cell phone attached to his thick belt. His job requires the safety vest and the equipment, and he is committed to the well-being of the district students. They know it, too. Some students trust him to the extent that they confide in him, both regarding personal concerns and potential criminal activity. Horton is straightforward and straight-talking with youth. One can see, however, that he could be overpowering if someone were not in sync with his goals.

Horton does not take his job lightly. It seems the job is tailored to his expertise and skills with young people; he takes pride in knowing by sight "pretty much" all the district students, and he knows the names of many in the schools he patrols. He is a tough professional, however, and no one would make the mistake of dismissing him as soft or easygoing. He is neither; instead, he means business. There's a straightforward, uncompromising toughness that is part of his personality. He seems ideally suited to the job he performs.

There is much to admire about a bulked-up safety officer who loves his job, doesn't mind walking a school beat, and is thoroughly dedicated to the students in these schools. He performs a service that should be *regulation* or *standard* in every school district nationwide. However, how many tough, uncompromising school officers are available who have students' safety and well-being as a daily goal? Gaining compliance of often surly students on a daily basis cannot be easy. Horton has mastered the art of the job to make it seem easy. And, of course, he wants every student he talks with on his beat to succeed. How good is that for youth!

16

SOCIAL
RESPONSIBILITY

Situations and events that require responses from members of a school community often occur in school settings. Take note of students' classroom, lunch area and assembly behavior, plus their attitudes and conversations, for example. One role educators and school leaders assume is that of sensitizing students to their obligations as members of a larger group, whether in the school building, on a playing field, while participating in a field trip, or when riding the bus to and from home. Parents may not necessarily devote attention to the topic of *social responsibility* unless an event occurs and their children mention it specifically or ask questions. The following situations might challenge students or heighten their awareness about social responsibility; these may serve as topics for class discussion.

1. Alana Matthews drops her pencil during a unit test, and in picking it up sees Todd Baker referring to a sheet of paper with notes. He carefully shoves it under his desk each time, but refers to it often during the test.

2. Mia Conley dislikes school; she is usually one of the very last students picked when group activities occur and team leaders choose their teammates. She and Mike Healy are noticeably left out. Mia is humiliated. The students seem to all know one another well, while she has no friends.

3. Tom Redwine is a student with good academic abilities, yet his physical looks draw students' mimicking and laughter. His unruly hair and shuffling walk, in addition to a bit of spittle that remains visible every time he speaks—and more so if he is excited or upset and speaking about something—have become known to many students in the school who look for him, ready to point and laugh.

4. Todd Dubose is a student who stands out because he routinely wears wrinkled or messy clothing that does not seem clean. He apparently does not own a variety of clothing, as do other students in the middle class community where the school is located. His manners yield to shouting out in class, yet he is not defiant or disruptive. He seems "rough around the edges," in sharp contrast to the majority of students.

5. Joel Snyder has been labeled *gay* by some students and he hates it. His family consists of his mother and her sister, Martha. They might influence Joel's tendency to prefer the company of women, since the boys in his class are merciless toward him. He is sensitive and sincere, and he respects others to the extent that he cannot shout back when he hears "gay" as he walks the school hallways.

Social responsibility in the context of schools comprises students' awareness of and respect for others, including teachers and all other school building adults as well as fellow students. Students hopefully will exhibit growth in sensitivity to others. All members of a school community, within and outside of classrooms, can expect students to show them respect. Students may need reminders, however, about sensitivity to others in the school community. These are individuals who accomplish specific tasks for the smooth, efficient operation of schools, though they may not be teachers or administrators or office staff members.

If we think about patrons' groups—such as patrons of the arts—as well as sponsors, community groups, business and merchants' groups, welfare leagues, political action groups, and boards and committees devoted to many causes, we understand that individuals work in groups to achieve goals and benefit communities across the country. A respectful, open, and sensitive approach to each person in a group is expected. This expectation applies to schools and all who attend school or carry out functions in and around the school building. The concept may need repeating year by year; if students hear the reminder, they may remember the meaning behind it. We are obligated to sensitize students to others in society, whether they share similarities with them or show differences of various kinds. In addition, though they may not realize it, no student wants to seem different among classmates, especially in grades 6 through 12.

Students' social responsibility also extends to their witnessing, or knowledge of, one or more students doing any of the following: cheating or lying; stealing, whether possessions or money; having someone else write an assigned paper or complete an assigned project; setting off a fire alarm or reporting a bomb threat; excluding others who are regarded as "unacceptable" in some way from a social clique; harassing or bullying or humiliating a student or a group of students; having awareness of a school or bus problem that exists yet doing nothing, telling no one, and "laughing it off"; ganging up in a group against a student; spreading rumors; or grabbing money, books, or other personal property from someone else on the bus, or inciting others to disruptive behavior that affects the driver's safety or close observation of traffic and road conditions.

Instructors may want to remind students that rules and procedures help create order in a building and in the classroom. Each class students attend will usually seem unique because of the subject matter, the methods of the instructor, the tone that is set, the expectations of students, and the interaction of students and teacher. Explain your welcoming their ideas about additional rules and procedures about social responsibility—that is, the awareness of and sensitivity to others in group situations, as they deem necessary. There is a social etiquette expected in group situations; you might mention juries and jury duty; social and community action groups; or school settings that may require group work.

Contexts and environments determine our responses, but we can become more aware of appropriate conduct, as well as thinking before speaking; listening to others with respect and acceptance of their point of view; and behaving in a neutral but open manner. Our goal is for students to understand the diversity of group situations and practice appropriate speech and behaviors, and for their actions to show respect toward others. We do not have to all think alike, but we must respect others, their backgrounds, their ideas, and their feelings.

READINESS

1. What approaches or discussion topics may help sensitize students to differences among groups of people? Might teachers routinely assemble diverse groups of students to complete learning activities in the classroom?

2. How can educators create a classroom atmosphere of respect and acceptance among students, despite any perceived differences? Creating this atmosphere might be a year-long, day-by-day effort. What student behaviors are your priorities? Specifying what you expect of students is a first step toward gaining their compliance.

3. Is it necessary for instructors to explain the differing levels of maturity that might account for some behaviors, different degrees of sensitivity, and varying attitudes among a room of students?

4. How do neutral behavior, a sense of fairness, and receptive listening help create tolerance and respect?

5. Recall conversations with parents or a counselor about students' understanding of others and their respect for fellow stu-

dents. What expectations do you have for students' speech, behavior, and actions toward those students who are perceived as "different"?

RESPONSIBILITY

1. Is it an instructor's responsibility to change the attitudes, habits, or speech of students who seem insensitive to others?
2. If we fail to teach students an awareness of and sensitivity to others' differences, what can we expect in terms of their conduct, attitudes, and interactions with others?
3. Schools grow larger and in many cases reflect diverse populations. How can we help to encourage sensitivity to and respect for others if these issues have not been addressed at home? Or will students exhibit the correct responses, including *tolerance* and *respect*, when necessary—for example, in a job setting?
4. Review any conversations you have had with parents about a child's respect or disrespect of others, and how the problem was handled. What was the reaction of the parent to whom you spoke?

RESPONSE

1. Does your school have a student code of conduct or rule(s) about sensitivity toward others? What does the code specify? Does it work?
2. What situations have you observed among students that challenged their sensitivity? Group work sometimes creates problems, yet solving a problem with others with a time limit can be an effective exercise in group dynamics. Learning about others' family customs and holidays might also expand one's understanding of differences, as well as of the similarities that exist among people despite divergent backgrounds.

3. Is it necessary to create a list of behaviors and expectations—especially highlighting *respect, sensitivity,* and *fair treatment*—and post it in each classroom? Are periodic reviews of these characteristics and behavior important? How have students reacted to these discussions?

4. What steps might instructors and school leaders take when students come to school unprepared—for example, their forms are unsigned by parents; there is a lack of phone accessibility; they have inadequate supplies for the classroom, though these supplies were required weeks ago; or they exhibit uncertainty about what is expected of them?

5. What challenges have you witnessed or experienced in terms of students' respect for one another, and how were the problems solved?

17

STUDENT BEHAVIORS AND ATTITUDES TOWARD ACADEMICS

Dr. Gloria Harding, unit district superintendent of Colchester County, reads the printout summary of responses as well as the lists of written comments compiled in a survey of the district teachers and staff members. The responders offer some unexpected and negative comments about students, which concerns the school leader.

In a discussion with her associate superintendent, Marlon Chambers, Harding insists, "Students in K–12 classes are usually responsive to instructors and class requirements. Like most students, ours benefit from encouragement of their efforts, and I know they seek out adults who show interest in their progress and also offer help to remedy any of their weaknesses."

Chambers pauses to think about the Colchester students' responsiveness to instruction and his impressions of the survey summary and conclusions. He offers this opinion: "One of my coaches said at the beginning of each season, 'Attitude is everything.' He was talking about sports. But that quote might apply to academics. Students' attitudes can affect their academic work. Students are also sensitive to teachers' attitudes, and our teachers verbalize what I see as high expectations of our students, Gloria."

The survey pinpoints district faculty members who perceive less overall student interest in both academics and extracurricular activities than in previous years. Respondents selected the choice, "Fewer students seem to exhibit genuine concern about completing course requirements," or "Students' sense of responsibility for learning and achieving seems more casual and, at times, occasional rather than continual or usual." (The latter item questioned professionals' impressions of student responses to potentially low or possibly failing grades in a specific class. However, responders also noted that a low grade or a series of low grades seemed to influence students' increased concern and subsequent increased effort.)

Harding is not one to linger when a problem surfaces, and she plans to engage the faculty in helping to "check on, and, if necessary, change" any nonproductive attitudes of students. Like all school leaders, this administrator seeks increased, if not maximum, student involvement in studying and in achieving grades commensurate with their individual abilities. In fact, the priority issues for all district professionals, starting immediately, will be taking steps to improve student attitudes; increasing students' school involvement in academics, as necessary; and enlisting all district teachers to expect and promote increased academic achievement on the part of all students. Harding also plans to draft a summary of the salient points in the survey and speak to faculty groups in their subject areas. She is especially interested in teachers' opinions and recommendations.

As a result of the meetings, groups of teachers provide feedback about some of their students. The attitude component is cited by one teacher who monitors a resource center for the students. She asks students about their academic subjects; one responds, "I don't like the maps and astronomy we do. I can't find anything." Another student reveals, "Math is okay—it's language arts I don't ever enjoy." And yet another student, in the high school, states, "There's no purpose for studying history. I'll be in business with my dad. I'll work on *cars*," he emphasizes. The teacher wonders if students' negativity is occasional and due to a low grade recently, or if it is a persistent pattern.

Students, including those quoted above, may be gifted with computer knowledge and ready for any task related to online challenges; yet many jobs and career fields still require workers with a well-rounded academic education that includes, but is not solely confined to, computer knowledge. Many jobs require employees to compose reports, letters, or memos, along with documenting instructions and procedures; the final product can be computer generated, but the best letter content comes from a worker's in-house experience and knowledge, as well as his or her communication skills.

Applying math skills, using logical reasoning and writing to answer specific customer complaints may also be necessary in many business settings. The analysis of specific mechanical operations and malfunctions is taken for granted in most business and industrial settings. In addition, knowledge of economics and geography helps businesspeople reach target customers and their businesses in all areas of the world, in addition to helping them advertise in areas where their products are needed.

Good reading skills seem to be necessary for a majority of employees as they review reports, articles, summaries, and responses to customers, for example. Thus, reading labs to help students review and master particular reading problems are available in most elementary classes, and supplemental review and enrichment of skills through junior and senior high school English classes and reading labs are also available.

On a daily basis, however, a teacher's attitude toward the material as well as toward all class members seems to be another factor in students' academic progress. Teachers who approach course content with a positive attitude and show interest in the progress of each student can change students' attitudes. An instructor's smile or laughter, plus encouragement while pointing to a key idea that stood out in the chapter—if no students mention that idea—may help students become more accustomed to reading and analyzing material, participating in discussions, and asking and answering questions in a group. These in-class practices may help students in their future employment, especially when reading or writing procedural manuals, for example.

By what other means can teachers change student attitudes? The breakout groups following the next meeting with Harding address the topic of *attitude* and reveal some specific ideas: Teachers might allow small student groups in class to list and share three or four jobs or careers that each student might want to pursue in the future, jobs requiring specific application of a school subject. Also, teachers might appoint groups in class to explain how to acquire and maintain the attitude of success that is needed for academic work, now and in the future, whether in college or the workplace. Students might be willing to share their academic experiences and outcomes. In addition, encouraging students to make a decision to succeed might be the first step toward a commitment to all the learning opportunities available to them, currently and throughout their schooling. That commitment might change any less-than-satisfactory attitudes and academic patterns.

Student behaviors may also change when students know what is expected of them and are sure about how to complete individual course assignments—these two expectations might require repetition and reminders—and when they know how to use the specific class materials designed to help them review and understand the concepts of each unit of study. Expectations that put the burden on students include completing study questions; contributing to reviews of specific sections or pages in the textbook for a quiz; taking class notes from group work and panels; and taking pretests that further stimulate thinking about the material covered.

Attitudes may change when students realize there are a variety of methods for reading, reviewing, discussing, and studying material. (These methods include whole-class review with students raising questions; small-group, question-and-answer panels; review of study questions and answers at home, explaining answers to an adult listener; raising questions in class for extra participation points and experiencing success with completed assignments; and compiling a series of notes and acquiring specific new knowledge. All these activities may lead to readiness for tests and quizzes.)

READINESS

1. Compile practice exercises and chapter study questions for all learning units.
2. Look for textbooks that present the material in different ways from the text students currently use; the new explanations and examples may help students.
3. Send the course of study objectives, as well as monthly assignment sheets, with each class day's subject matter, to parents.
4. Teach students how to study for your subject area; use the book to guide students' note-taking. Offer a review of how to outline a chapter or isolate key topics and supporting ideas. (This may also comprise a student's worksheet guide for test reviews.)
5. Exchange ideas and suggestions with other instructors to acquire new materials and approaches to course readings, activities, and objectives.
6. Teach the terms and specific vocabulary words unique to each textbook chapter. Teach the curriculum goals using supplementary exercises to review material and/or remedy students' gaps in learning. You may need a variety of approaches and explanations for some students and additional worksheets or practice exercises.

RESPONSIBILITY

1. If students are unwilling to complete remedial or additional work or the exercises for review and mastery, or if they are unwilling to attend tutorial sessions, call parents and also contact the students' counselors. You will need to know individual students' problems in order to help them.

2. Allow a counselor or advisor to intervene if the tutorial sessions seem like a penalty to a student.

3. Monitor each student's progress in mastering the course's goals. Relearning helps students catch up and move along with the rest of the class.

4. Identify any pattern of weakness that may be common among a group of students, a "missing link" of knowledge in the subject matter previously taught. Plan a unit to review and/or reteach that missing block of skills or knowledge.

RESPONSE

1. Center classroom study on skills students need to know (e.g., locating a main idea or topic sentence, along with reviewing facts or proofs to support the idea or topic; identifying a conclusion or summary in the material assigned).

2. Allow students to review these skills and practice them in small groups assigned to specific textbook sections, or after reading and discussing articles or chapters not in their textbooks.

3. Remedy student weaknesses: Is there a learning lab for individualized help, or are tutors available? What supplemental exercises might you provide to tailor grade-level objectives to students' needs for each unit of study? Anticipate and plan for future learning units throughout the year.

4. Schedule regular meetings with subject-area teachers to exchange approaches, worksheets, practice tests, chapter outlines, and other aids, to encourage students' success with the material.

5. Enlist parents' help with calls and notes home about the requirements of the class and the daily work necessary. (Attach the assignment sheet or the calendar for the month's work and topic.)

6. Encourage students' efforts toward mastery of new knowledge (as shown by a test or worksheet) or learning the grade-

level/subject-level objectives. Call homes with positive news about students' progress.

7. Review study techniques, effective note taking, and how to use notes to review for tests; allow student groups to create review questions about each chapter and each unit. Include a discussion of how the material reaches beyond the text, to current events or skills required in specific careers or jobs.

18

RESPONSES TO AN INDIVIDUAL WHO TALKS ABOUT DESTRUCTIVE ACTS IN A SCHOOL SETTING

Raul Pellman and Alva Meade have known one another since first grade: they live within a few blocks of each other. Both are easygoing, and each has helped the other in a number of ways, even loaning small amounts of money if needed. Neither has a relationship with a girl currently, but both have talked about whom they prefer and would like to date from school.

But Alva notices a change in his friend which he does not understand: Raul talks about setting off a small bomb or firecrackers in their high school. His reason? Raul casually says, "Let's just see what happens." He has also mentioned calling in a false fire alarm or reporting that he has seen "a guy wearing a mask and holding a gun right out in the quadrangle" of the school.

Alva, at first surprised, has now indicated to Raul that he is not interested and doesn't want to talk about bombs, firecrackers, or guys with guns, nor, as he has indicated more recently, to hear about them. Raul will indeed switch the subject to something else, yet he returns to it. Alva is also tired of Raul's "Boom! Boom! Keee-boom!" followed by laughter. So often has he heard the "routine," as he calls it, that he now wants to avoid Raul. This pattern in Raul's talk may lead to the end of their comfortable friendship—they've always gone to games and events together and could count on each other for opinions and advice.

Some students may harbor fears as a result of widely publicized school shootings—one may have occurred in their own state—as well as school disruptions such as fights, or gang members shaking down students; those fears may be dispelled with humor, which might explain Raul's "Boom!" noises, as though the subject is funny. If he talks about a disruptive event as a joke, he may feel he is in control of his fears on some level.

On the other hand, some students talk about potential destruction or violence to fellow students in order to *test* someone, to gauge the response. Might Raul want a partner in crime? In this case, Alva has made it clear he doesn't want to hear about it because he doesn't want to get in trouble. He reminds his friend that expulsion from school and a police record will follow any violence or destruction perpetrated in school for the rest of Raul's life. Still, Raul seems to continue joking about the subject.

READINESS

1. A school safety officer directs and manages safe school efforts. He knows the students by sight (and many, of course, by name) and would help or give advice to any student who approached him.
2. Each school's security team drafts a plan of action in response to emergency events, including a student with a gun on-site; a fight that sets one group against another; an altercation during a game with a rival school; a verbal argument among students in a gym class that threatens to involve all class members; and any potential threat of a serious nature requiring response. The document's contents will be shared and discussed with adults in a school building.

3. Schoolwide practices occur during the school year, timing students for safe but efficient exiting of the building; expectations of appropriate student behavior are clearly stated.
4. School policies define penalties for planning or carrying out any events that threaten the security and safety of any members of the school community.
5. Local newspapers inform readers in the district of the safe-school practices under way, as well as the presence of a school safety officer and the support of local police personnel—as a deterrent, for example.
6. Members of the community are willing to join a safe schools team (as needed) to arrive at a school for practice of safety drills and to fulfill their designated roles (monitoring students or checking attendance, as needed; allaying fears; leading students to a designated safe place on or off campus; or any other responsibility necessary).
7. "Safe schools" assemblies review the need for all students to remain alert to safety issues; to cooperate during practice exiting drills; and to become familiar with safe school policies and updates thereof. Students create a film or presentation to review school rules and procedures related to safety.
8. Students realize their responsibility to discourage friends and classmates from viewing safety efforts as humorous, and to express disapproval of any suggestions about compromising school safety efforts and rules.
9. Adult monitors are on duty in all hallways and at all building entrances throughout each school day.

RESPONSIBILITY

1. School administrators take safe school measures very seriously and will send reports to students' homes should they suggest that safety efforts are "ridiculous," as one student said, or if students joke about the safety of the building and grounds. A

referral also is sent to the students' counselors, the dean of students, and the safety officer. The dean or safety officer meets with the student and/or a student's parents in all instances of students regarding safety measures as less serious than they should.

2. All students understand that they are responsible for their own safety as well as that of others. Each student might sign his agreement with a statement of the school's safety plan or a pledge to avoid joking about safety issues on-site, if joking has occurred. Included are the expectations that students will cooperate with adults in all safety-emergency situations; that they will exit a building promptly per instructions; and that they will report suspicious or unusual activities related to safety anywhere on school property.

3. Designation of a School Safety Week, featuring guest speakers for students, occurs yearly. The speakers (e.g., police personnel, private security guards, parking lot monitors, administrators who review safety measures in their own schools) describe their safety experiences and priorities. The follow-up may include incorporating student suggestions for further safety measures, a student school-safety panel, a safety poster campaign and competition, a school safety slogan, and similar activities.

4. A Student Safety Committee, as discussed by the safety panel for Safety Week, is considered; the committee would receive students' suggestions and questions, plus plan programs with follow-up activities periodically throughout the year.

RESPONSE

1. Students avoid individuals or groups who converse about potential disruptive events, especially on school property. The best student response is to indicate a refusal to discuss illegal or unsafe practices on school property. Reporting concerns to counselors or Safe School Committee members is mandatory.

An alternative is sending an anonymous note about what has been heard from students that might compromise school-safety efforts.

2. School leaders encourage safe schools practices, especially by rewarding students for reporting concerns such as an unlocked door, a light bulb missing in a dim corridor, the lack of a monitor or supervisor in a building area that might need one, and so on.

3. The Safe School Committee accepts recommendations from the school safety officer. One such recommendation might be to hire a parking lot monitor if a number of student cars at the high school have been broken into. The monitor would utilize a golf-cart-style vehicle. The year-round position would require professional experience in designing, managing, or executing safety tasks.

4. The school safety policy and practices document is revised and updated each year, as needed, utilizing data or input from the Safe School Committee, faculty, staff, students, and parents and community members who are interested in and/or trained in safety assessment and management.

5. Safe School Committee members are allowed to visit other schools, assessing their policies and practices as well as their concerns. (Budget limits may compromise adding safety features—exploration of grants for funding is strongly encouraged.)

6. Faculty, staff, and students remain alert to safety practices; for instance, keeping classroom doors open when a class is not meeting. Lock empty classrooms. Other issues are rumors and how to handle them; how to deal with an unfamiliar student present in the building; and how to be ready to notice anything out of the ordinary—for example, a noise in a gym when no class is scheduled or the strong smell of a noxious substance.

19

TEENS' VIOLENCE
AGAINST TEENS

Three friends walked a nature trail recently, and one of them shot and killed one of his companions. The shooter and his friend dumped the body in a wooded area off the walking path. A motive for the crime has not been publicized.

A home security camera captured an event, later aired on national television, that was difficult to watch. A group of teens, males and females, appear in one of their homes. Prior to this, one of the group had engaged in an ongoing but phony e-mail friendship with one of the other teens. One of the perpetrators locks the door after the arrival of the girl who has been tricked; and, suddenly, several of the teens, taking turns, beat her about the head and face at close range. They corner her so that she cannot escape, ignoring her repeated pleas with them, one after another, to stop beating her. Her injuries are severe, despite the fact that she tries to cover her face and continues pleading. Apparently, all she had done was believe the e-mail friendship was genuine, as well as coming to this home.

Although others are implicated in this third event, it is a group of four teens—one aged eighteen; two, seventeen; and one, sixteen—who confess to having used duct tape to suffocate a fifth teen, aged eighteen. One of the seventeen-year-olds is female. The dead teen, wrapped in a plastic bag, was left in the home of one of the perpetrators. They planned the crime.

In yet another incident, a group of three males—one aged seventeen and two aged sixteen—were charged with assault when they beat up a fifteen-year-old male after lifting the youth, then throwing him on the ground. They punched his face so severely he had to undergo extensive facial surgery. No reason was given for the assault.

It seems unfathomable: friends savagely beating up a student they know or even beating, then killing, the victim. These crimes were not committed by gang members. And it appears all knew their victims. Are these violent teens angry or disturbed? Have they utilized the hunt-and-kill computer games that pit a viewer against an unknown enemy, and thus become desensitized to taking another person's life? U.S. laws hold these perpetrators accountable; perhaps none felt they would be caught.

Why did each of these groups of students continue their brutality when at least one victim, that we know of, pleaded with them to stop? From the standpoint of any viewer of the security video, seeing and hearing the teen's pleas during the repeated attacks was horrifying; and it was very difficult to continue watching, as the perpetrators remained cold, distant, and uncaring.

Teens dislike rules, restraints, and the regulations they are told they must follow, whether these are school or home rules. Yet the current cohort of young adults seems to be the most privileged and secure generation in this country's history. Parents are, for the vast majority of teens, motivated to give their children whatever they want. On the other hand, have teens been negatively influenced by movies, recording stars, entertainers, and actors? Are these good role models for young adults? Also, what effect might music and movies espousing violence have on teens? Most teens want total freedom from any restraints. The cases of teens beating up and killing students their age reveal students' unfathomable group violence and cool, calm savagery. How do we teach them to use their privileges and freedom wisely?

And yet, these young adults bristle when they interpret consequences and results of their choices as "unfair." Teens currently are quick to see and judge what is "fair" and "unfair." How many times have you heard young people exclaim "That's not fair!"? Whatever they are referring to must rule out in their own thinking the unfair nature of beating or killing another teen. What could provoke their taking another's life?

Is the problem with their choices connected to the freedom they have to do whatever they want most of the time? Few school administrators and teachers indulge young adults. Has this fact driven them to violent behaviors against others? What is bothering teens? Is their freedom a double-edged sword in that teens may not be taught how to *use* their freedom? How do we teach them accountability after the facts reveal how teens may use their freedoms?

READINESS

1. Clear, forceful school policies and expectations specifying appropriate behavior from students, especially in junior and senior high school, set up standards of conduct for young adults at the times of their lives when teens need guidelines and restrictions. What standards is it necessary to set for teens' appropriate behavior, choices, and interactions with fellow students and adults? For example, one expectation of all students is that they show respect (both verbal and behavioral) for others in the school, and during activities and sports events.

2. Parents need to know the school's rules, whether disseminated by letter from a school leader or dean or published in the local newspaper. The rules might also become a discussion topic in classes. What rules of behavior and speech do you suggest a school leader might specify in print for all to read, discuss, and adhere to?

3. What is an appropriate penalty for assault of another student— or for joining a group whose members threaten or intend to carry out violence?

4. What penalties should follow affrays on school property and other specific student behaviors that may occur routinely in some students' school careers? What penalty might follow defiance of authority, for example? What penalty needs to be set for inappropriate behavior or for using unsuitable language on buses?

RESPONSIBILITY

1. A school resource officer or a member of the local police force might offer insights about students' behaviors and infractions in grades 7 through 12, not only locally, but nationally. A partnership between a school district and local police might be of mutual benefit, and the insights and experiences exchanged helpful in creating or refining school policies and practices. Drawing parent groups into the partnership might also be considered.

2. A listing of local resource persons who might help a school team or committee establish policies specifying appropriate student behavior, as well as deterrents to inappropriate choices, could be set up. Also, the use of local counseling professionals as resources could be considered. Parents may wish to consult local personnel with their concerns and questions about the growth stages of their youth.

3. A school psychologist might offer additional insights about adolescents' growth toward maturity, as well as deviations from norms and proximate causes of deviations. A letter sent home to parents outlining the school psychologist's role in students' lives, as needed, along with a list of issues that appear to trouble students in grades 6 through 12, might serve as reminders should any problems occur. Or the school professional might write a year-long series of newspaper articles or columns about students' defiance of authority, inappropriate language, disrespectful behavior toward one another, and so forth.

4. Faculty and staff may need to review professional literature devoted to the psychological changes that occur as students ex-

perience growth stages during grades 6 through 12, and to the techniques that can be used to diffuse their anger or the steps that can be initiated to discourage any disruption of classes or defiance of school personnel.

RESPONSE

1. Might the guidance department personnel maintain a record of professional contacts who have assisted specific students in past grades, whether a school psychologist, a private therapist, or a social worker?

2. A school code of conduct in paragraph form, with clear expectations for student behavior, might be included in the student handbook—and reviewed and updated yearly. A committee which includes student representatives might also offer an insider's perspective about some behaviors adults might not be aware of.

3. The student handbook might outline warnings about recurrences of individual students' behaviors that may threaten their school career, if not graduation. Fighting, engaging in class disruptions, refusal to adhere to school rules or the instructions of building adults, defiance of authority, and similar problems deserve mention in print. Also, students might need to expect that parental input with a dean and principal will be necessary in order to reinstate a student in school once he or she has been suspended.

4. Parents and teachers might initiate conferences with a student in the school setting to review and suggest necessary changes in behavior—whether the issue is lack of cooperation with adults, verbal bullying of students, challenging other students with threats, or persistent and menacing hostility. A contract to encourage change in a student's behavior, indicating specific new behaviors that must be seen in a student in order to reinstate the pupil in school, may be considered a first step.

ABOUT THE AUTHOR

Helen M. Sharp writes about improving educational efforts for K–12 students, both inside and outside school classrooms. Two of her recent books, for example, center on contemporary school crisis events, specifically directed to potential as well as current administrators. A licensed school administrator, Sharp has contributed more than fifty articles and book reviews in the field of education administration as well as five books.